Commentary
On
1 & 2
Thessalonians

Designed to be
helpful to Bible Class
Teachers

by Leon Crouch

IBSN: 0-89137-138-9

Table of Contents

Preface ii
Introduction 1
1 Thessalonians
    Chapter 1 11
    Chapter 2 26
    Chapter 3 47
    Chapter 4 61
    Chapter 5 78

2 Thessalonians 97
    Chapter 1 104
    Chapter 2 115
    Chapter 3 132
Bibliography 143

Preface

During the past 30 years there has been a renewed interest in the study of the Thessalonian Epistles. The most likely reason for this renewed interest in these two short documents is the upsurge of interest in eschatology. It seems that many of the recent studies from these letters have been designed to further some special theory about something connected with the end time. The theories about the so-called rapture are almost totally based on some statements in these epistles. Also a lot of time and effort has been used to speculate about the "man of sin" and his work from statements in these writings. Much of the argument about whether Paul thought he would still be alive at the return of Christ is centered in these two epistles. It is my hope that this brief study will point out some of the extremes which should be avoided, and make some valid suggestions about Paul's teaching which will be helpful to the reader.

The main reason for the approach of this study is to give Bible class teachers a reasonable statement of Paul's teaching which is based solidly on the text yet not too technical to be useful. The study is based on the American Standard Version of 1901. However, my study has considered each word in the Greek text as the commentary will demonstrate.

My genuine thanks are expressed to the many helps and sources used in preparation for writing. Several individuals have helped in reading the text and making valuable comments. The faults which are still in the work are mine. To my wife, Peggy, special thanks are given for her constant help and encouragement while I was writing. My thanks also to Bennie Whitehead for the invitation to write and for all at Quality Publications for their work in putting it all together in a useful form.

Leon Crouch

Introduction

While apparently traveling to the province of Asia, the apostle Paul and his companions were hindered by the Holy Spirit from continuing in that direction. They planned then to go into Bithynia but the Spirit stopped them again. They continued their journey until they arrived at Troas. During the night a vision appeared to Paul in which a man from Macedonia appealed to him, "Come over into Macedonia, and help us" (Acts 16:6-9 ASV). Paul and his co-workers, Silas, Timothy, Luke and perhaps others, traveled over to Europe and stopped in Philippi. From Luke's account of the stay in Philippi, it is clear that the preaching was successful. Lydia and her household, along with the jailer and his household were obedient to the gospel (Acts 16:14,15,30-34). The stay in Philippi ended with Paul and Silas being released from jail with what may be called an apology from the officials. They asked them to leave the city.

Paul, along with Silas and Timothy, traveled along the Egnatian Way, the great military and commercial highway that linked the Aegean with the Adriatic. They passed Amphipolis, about 30 miles southwest of Philippi, and on some 28 miles to Apollonia, and about 40 miles further along the highway they came to Thessalonica (Acts 17:1). Since Paul was evidently interested in preaching in the largest and most important cities, they found a synagogue of the Jews and stayed there for a time.

The City of Thessalonica

Location: Thessalonica was the largest and most important city in Macedonia. It was the regional seat of the Roman administration in the century before Christ. In addition to being located on the Egnatian Way, the city had a magnificent harbor. The city was located at the northernmost point of the Thermaic Gulf, a short distance east of the mouth of the Axius river. Its situation gave it some natural advantages which were augmented by the art of men. It was an important city in Paul's day and continues to be today both politically and commercially. No doubt the strategic position of Thessalonica was the reason Paul and his co-workers were guided there to preach the gospel.

History: Strabo, a well-known Greek geographer, says that Thessalonica was founded in 315 B.C. by the Macedonian general Cassender, who named the city after his wife. The wife was the daughter of Philip and stepsister of Alexander the Great. It was first settled by refugees from a large number of smaller towns in the area which had been destroyed by war. In 167 B.C., Macedonia was divided into four districts and Thessalonica was made the capital of the second division. The influence of the city continued to grow when the area was made a Roman province. During the second civil war between Caesar and Pompey (42 B.C.) Thessalonica remained loyal to Anthony and Octavian. As a reward the city was given the status of a free city. This gift allowed the city to appoint its own magistrates, who were given the unusual title of politarchs (Acts 17:6,8). Since the term politarch does not appear in earlier Greek literature, some have accused Luke of making a mistake. However, the term has been found in an inscription on the Vardar Gate at the western boundary of the city and in other inscriptions from the area. There are some nineteen of these inscriptions dating from the second century B.C. to the third century A.D., being used for the most part for magistrates in Macedonian cities. Five of the inscriptions refer to Thessalonica itself which early on had five politarchs and at a later time, six.[1]

Population: Most of the people of Thessalonica were Greeks. Mainly because of its political status the city remained to a large extent Greek in character. There were a few Romans and a few Orientals there in the first century, and because of the attractive commercial prospects of the area, there was a rather large Jewish population. The Jews were apparently active in their religious practices because there was a large number of Gentile "God-fearers" who attended the synagogue, together with quite a few socially prominent women. The Gentiles were apparently attracted to the lofty ethical monotheism of the Jews and attended the imageless worship of the synagogue without becoming full proselytes. When Paul arrived in Thessalonica, the city was already filled with diverse religious groups in addition to the Jewish synagogue. The Egyptian divinities Isis, Serapis, and Osiris were well established in the city. Also the Greek cult of Dionysus and Cabiri were very popular.[2] However, the first converts in Thessalonica came from the synagogue (Acts 17:4; but cf. 1 Thessalonians 1:9).

Christianity Introduced Into Thessalonica:

Christianity came to this important city because of a divine intervention, it seems (Acts 16:6ff.). No doubt the Lord knew that there were people in this city who would accept the gospel and who would be traveling to various parts of the Empire taking the gospel with them.

When the preachers arrived at Thessalonica, they went to the synagogue where Paul "for three sabbath days reasoned with them from the scriptures, opening and alleging that it behooved the Christ to suffer, and to rise again from the dead." He argued that the Jesus whom he preached "is the Christ" (Acts 17:3). The success of the preaching stirred the jealousy of the Jews who gathered some "vile fellows of the rabble" and started a riot (Acts 17:5). They went to the house of Jason where Paul was staying, but when they could not find the apostle, they dragged Jason and some other Christians before the city officials. The claim was made that Paul was guilty of acting contrary to the decrees of Caesar because he preached another king, Jesus. That very night Paul was sent out of Thessalonica and made his way to Beroea (Acts 17:6-10). The extent of the hostility of the Jews in Thessalonica is seen in the fact that when they learned that Paul was preaching in

Beroea they went there and stirred up the crowds against him (Acts 17:13).

Length of stay: The mention that Paul preached in Thessalonica "for three sabbath days" has caused much speculation about the length of time he spent in that city. Was he there only for three weeks as might be suggested by mentioning three sabbath days? Or was he there longer? The evidence indicates a longer stay. It would most likely take longer than three weeks to mature the congregation to the point that their faith had "become an ensample to all that believe in Macedonia and in Achaia" (1 Thessalonians 1:7). Paul also mentions that he worked for his own support so as not to burden the Thessalonians (1 Thessalonians 2:9). It is also mentioned that the Philippian Christians had sent help to Paul. The text says that when Paul had departed from Macedonia no church helped except the Philippians, "for even in Thessalonica ye sent once and again to my needs" (Philippians 4:15-16). If that congregation sent twice to help Paul while he was in Thessalonica, he was most likely there longer than three weeks. It should be noted, however, that the passage in Philippians may mean that those Christians sent help to him both in Thessalonica and repeatedly elsewhere — once when he was in Thessalonica and more times when he was in other places. It is very possible that after three sabbaths in the synagogue, Paul was forced to preach elsewhere as happened in Ephesus (Acts 19,8,9). The fact that there were aspects of Christian truth about which Paul had to write later may indicate a shorter period in Thessalonica. The evidence is not conclusive as to the length of time spent in this city. It may have been no longer than a month or as much as three months.

Authenticity of First Thessalonians:

Very few have questioned that Paul wrote 1 Thessalonians. Some who followed the extreme views of the Tubingen school have done so. Also the radical Dutch school of Van Manen rejected all of the Pauline epistles. The evidence for 1 Thessalonians outside the epistle is not as early nor as strong

4

as for some of the other writings of Paul. There is some evidence that Ignatius (about 117 A.D.) knew the epistle as did Polycarp, a few years later. Irenaeus, in his *Against Heresies* 5:30, is the earliest to mention it by name. Clement of Alexandria is the first of the so-called Fathers to attribute the work to Paul. It is found in both the canon of Marcion, about 140 A.D.; the Muratorian canon, about 170 A.D. and in the early Syrian and Latin versions. The evidence in the epistle is very clear. Two times the author claims to be Paul (1:1; 2:18). A comparison of the account in Acts with 1 Thessalonians will show that they are not contradictory, but can be harmonized and it takes both to get the full story. The vocabulary and style are in harmony with Pauline authorship.

It is recognized today that the objections that have been made against the authenticity of 1 Thessalonians are inadequate or even baseless. There is no valid reason for questioning this epistle as genuine.

Place and Date of First Thessalonians:

Place: When Paul left Thessalonica he went to Beroea and on to Athens. While in Athens the apostle became very concerned about the young Christians in Thessalonica so he sent Timothy back "to establish" and "comfort" them (1 Thessalonians 3:1,2). After preaching in Athens for a short period, Paul went to Corinth (Acts 18:1). While in Corinth, Timothy came to him (Acts 18:5). It is generally agreed that shortly after the arrival of Timothy with news from Thessalonica, the three who had first worked there joined in writing 1 Thessalonians (1 Thessalonians 1:1). Corinth, then, is the place of writing. The note in the King James Version which says the writing took place in Athens is to be rejected. Remember that such notes were added by men and are not a part of the inspired text.

Date: There are few events in the life of Paul which can be fixed with any certainty. The work of Paul at Corinth is one of the most certain contacts with secular history. Gallio was proconsul in Corinth at the time (Acts 18:11-18). An inscription at Delphi in central Greece dates a proclamation of the

Emperor Claudius some time early in A.D. 52. Gallio is mentioned as proconsul of Asia at the time which means that Gallio had most likely started his term in the summer of A.D. 51. The trial of Paul before Gallio seems to have been early in Gallio's term in office. This assumption is based on the Jews' attempt to take advantage of his inexperience (Acts 18:12,13). If that is true, and it probably is, Paul would have left Corinth in the late summer or early fall of A.D. 51. Since he had spent about eighteen months there (Acts 18:11,18), he most likely had arrived late in A.D. 49 or early A.D. 50.

Timothy had returned to Thessalonica and then rejoined Paul in Corinth. This trip most likely had taken only a few months, but enough time passed that their faith was known in several places (1 Thessalonians 1:8,9). Also, some of the members had died (1 Thessalonians 4:13). From late summer of A.D. 50 to the spring of A.D. 51 is sufficient time for these things to have happened. The time of writing may be placed in the spring of A.D. 51 with reasonable confidence. At most it would be one year off.

Occasion for Writing:

After the abrupt departure from Thessalonica, Paul was very anxious about the fate of the young Christians there. He undoubtedly knew that they would become the target of the hatred of the enemies of truth. Would they be strong enough to endure was no doubt the question on his mind. He attempted to return to Thessalonica on two occasions but was somehow hindered (1 Thessalonians 2:17,18). He did send Timothy to them to learn if "the tempter had tempted" them and whether his labor among them had been in vain (1 Thessalonians 3:5). When Timothy returned, he brought information which was partly good and partly unsatisfactory. This mixed information motivated Paul to write this first epistle.

Timothy's report was mostly good. In spite of cruel persecution the faith of the Christians in Thessalonica had not been shaken, their love for one another was still strong and they continued to love Paul and desired to see him again

(1 Thessalonians 3:6). On the other hand, Timothy reported that Paul's teaching about the coming of the Lord had been misunderstood in part. The expectation of a quick return of the Lord had led some to give up their daily work and they had become dependent on the others for daily needs (1 Thessalonians 4:11; cf. 2 Thessalonians 3:6,8,10-12). Others among them were in despair over some of their number who had died, and whom they thought had missed out on the promised blessings expected at Christ's return (1 Thessalonians 4:13ff.).

Paul wrote this epistle to express his joy and thankfulness because of the faithfulness of the Christians in Thessalonica in the midst of persecutions, and also to help correct the misunderstandings among them.

Teaching in 1 Thessalonians:

It was not Paul's intention to give instruction on any one doctrine or to correct any one error. He did want to complete the teaching on the end time which had apparently been curtailed by a rather quick exit from the city. The first epistle is an evangelist's words to his recent converts in which references to doctrines are incidental. However, that fact makes these doctrines significant. Note the following points.

God

This epistle places great emphasis on the doctrine of God as contrasted with the false gods of the pagans. He is the One who has chosen His people (1:4), and who is the object of their faith (1:8) as the living and true God to whom they have turned (1:9). He is the One in whom they find ground for boldness (2:2), the One from whom they had been entrusted with the gospel (2:4), and it is His will that must be done (4:3; 5:18). The authors refer to God as "Father" in a way that indicates the term was in general use (1:1; 3:11; 3:13). God is the One who raised Jesus from the dead and who will bring His people from the dead (4:14,16), and who will consummate the salvation to which He has appointed them (5:9).

7

Jesus Christ

The Christology of 1 Thessalonians is high. The writers make spontaneous and almost unconscious references to Christ so that He is associated with God the Father in a way that shows Christ's deity (1:3; 3:11). He is called "Lord" (1:1; 2:1), a term used of God in Jewish circles. Christ is closely associated with the Father in the events of the end time (3:13; 4:16,17; 5:2) as well as in daily affairs of life (3:11,12). Jesus Christ died for believers (5:10) and delivers His followers from the wrath to come (1:10). Eternal life with Christ is the goal of Christian hope (4:17).

The Holy Spirit

References to the Holy Spirit are few in 1 Thessalonians, but His presence is obvious throughout the epistle. The gospel is preached by His power (1:5). His joy is given to those who believe His word (1:6), and He Himself is given to the believer (4:8). Paul and his co-workers also pleaded with the readers not to quench the Spirit (5:19).

Christian Living

First Thessalonians gives good insight into the life style God expects for His people. Their lives should be consistent with the gospel message, marked by their "work of faith and labor of love and patience of hope" (1:3). Some specific aspects of Christian ethics are mentioned as the context demands. For example, endurance under trial (2:14-16), love for one another (3:12), moral purity (4:3-8), honesty (4:11,12), and doing good to all people (5:15). The ultimate goal is sanctification of the complete person (5:23).

The End Time

By far the most attention is given to teaching about the end time in 1 Thessalonians. The coming of Christ and the accompanying resurrection along with various matters related to these events receive special emphasis. It is out of this emphasis that much recent study of the Thessalonian epistles has developed.

After Paul left Thessalonica, some of the converts to Christianity had died and their loved ones were filled with anxiety and wonder about the dead. The apostle gives assurance that the living Christians will have no advantage over the ones who had died when Jesus comes. The dead will be raised before anything happens to the living Christians. Then the two groups, those who have died and the ones still living, will be taken up to meet the Lord in the air. Both groups will be with Him forever (4:13-18). Following these words of assurance, the Thessalonian Christians are urged to live so that they will be ready for Christ's coming whenever it occurs (5:1-11). The coming of Christ is referred to near the end of each chapter in this epistle (1:10; 2:19; 3:13; 4:15-17; 5:23).

Each of these points of emphasis will be developed more as the specific verses are discussed. Special attention will be given to the word "presence" or "coming" and to the teaching in 4:13-18 because of the controversy about these concepts.

OUTLINE OF FIRST THESSALONIANS

I. Salutation, 1:1
II. Review of the History of the Thessalonian church, 1:2-10
    A. Their faithfulness, 1:2-3
    B. Their reception of the gospel exemplary, 1:4-7
    C. They had been active in sounding out the Word, 1:8-10
III. The Relationship of the Writers to the Church, 2:1-3:13
    A. The proper motive in preaching, 2:1-4
    B. The proper conduct in daily living, 2:5-12
    C. The preaching was the word of God, 2:13-16
    D. Concern for the church, 2:17-3:1-10
        1. Paul's desire to return, 2:17-20
        2. Timothy sent to help them, 3:1-5
        3. Timothy's report, 3:6-10
    E. Paul's prayer, 3:11-13
IV. Instructions About How to Live, 4:1-5:11
    A. The problem of sexual morality, 4:1-8
    B. The problem of social conduct, 4:9-12

9

    C. The problem about those who had died, 4:13-18

    D. The certainty of Christ's coming, 5:1-11

V. General Exhortations, 5:12-22

    A. Appeal for harmony among the Christians, 5:12-15

    B. Appeal for steadfastness, 5:16-22

VI. Conclusion, 5:23-28

NOTES

[1]E. D. Burton, "The Politarchs," in *American Journal of Theology* ii (1898), 598ff.; "Thessalonica," in *Baker Encyclopedia of the Bible*, ed. Walter A. Elwell (Grand Rapids, Michigan: Baker Book House, 1988), 2:2056.

[2]Abraham J. Malherbe, *Paul and the Thessalonians* (Philadelphia: Fortress Press, 1987), 6.

Chapter 1

TEXT AND EXPOSITION

I. SALUTATION, 1:11

V:1. Paul, and Silvanus, and Timothy, unto the church of the Thessalonians in God the Father and the Lord Jesus Christ: Grace to you and peace.

V:1 Paul,—According to the custom of first century letter writing, the author(s) are mentioned at the first. Paul is joined in the writing by "Silvanus" and "Timothy." It seems best to assume that these two were joined with Paul as giving consent and support to what he was sending to the Thessalonian Christians since they had helped in the establishment of that church. It is true that the plural pronoun is used often but in some places it seems almost certainly to refer to Paul only (Cf, 1 Thessalonians 3:1). The point to keep in mind is that Paul is basically responsible for the contents of the epistle.

This Paul is the same as the man called Saul in Acts (7:58; 8:1,3; etc.). This is a Jewish name and means "to ask" or "to pray." Paul is the Greek name which is used most of the time after Acts 13:9. Paul means "little" and evidently gave rise to several comments about his size. There is no way to know if the comments are true.

and Silvanus,—This person is the same as the Silas in the Book of Acts. He was one of the men spoken of as "chief men

11

among the brethren" (Acts 15:22). He was chosen to accompany Paul and Barnabas from Jerusalem to Antioch with the letter concerning Gentile believers. Later as preparations were being made for the second preaching journey, Paul refused to take John Mark. As a result Barnabas and John Mark went to Cyprus and Paul took Silas back to Galatia and on to Europe and Thessalonica. It is this journey that gives the background for this epistle. It is interesting that after this journey was over, Silvanus is mentioned only one other time in the New Testament (1 Peter 5:12).

and Timothy,—Timothy was from Lystra and is first mentioned in Acts 16:1ff. He was half Jew having a Greek father and a Jewish mother. His grandmother, Lois, and his mother, Eunice, were devout Jews and gave Timothy an education in the Scriptures (2 Timothy 1:5; 3:15). He apparently did not have two names since he is always called Timothy, a word meaning "honoring God." No doubt the name was given in hope that he would fulfill its meaning. While still young, perhaps about 17, Timothy began traveling with Paul. He proved to be a faithful worker and Paul sent him on various missions: to Macedonia, Acts 19:22; to Corinth, 1 Corinthians 4:17; and to Philippi, Philippians 2:19. He is also associated with Paul in the opening of six of his letters (2 Corinthians, Philippians, Colossians, Philemon, 1 and 2 Thessalonians). It seems very likely that he was with Paul in the beginning of the work in Thessalonica although it is not definitely stated.

unto the church of the Thessalonians—As is normal in the address of a first century letter, the names of the authors are followed by a description of the recipients of the letter. Here they are "the church of the Thessalonians" (Cf. 2 Thessalonians 1:1). This exact form of address is not found elsewhere in the New Testament. The words direct attention to the fact that the recent converts in Thessalonica now constitute a church, an *ekklesia*. The reference is not to a normal assembly for city business, but it is to the *ekklesia* of God.

in God the Father and the Lord Jesus Christ:—The church under consideration is the one which is "in" (Greek: *en*) a special relationship with God and Jesus Christ. Some such description was needed to make clear whose *ekklesia* it is to which they now belong. The mention of God first indicates that the church was nonheathen and the mention of Jesus Christ marks it as non-Jewish.

It is important to notice the close relationship between God and Christ in this statement. In Greek usage the preposition "in" before the word "God" and omitting it before the words "Lord Jesus Christ" indicates that Paul places God and Christ on an equal level. To speak of Jesus Christ in this way at this early date is very important because it proves the deity of Christ was not a late doctrinal development. Also, the two names, God and Christ, are used as proper names—a fact made clear by the absence of the definite article (the) in the Greek text. The combination of the human name, "Jesus," given to Him in response to the instructions of Gabriel (Luke 1:31; Matthew 1:21), with the title "Christ," the Greek form of the expected Messiah, and the title "Lord," the normal word for Jehovah, or LORD, in the Septuagint (Greek) version of the Old Testament, present a very high view of this person. He can properly be considered Deity, or God, with all the implications of these words.

Grace to you and peace.—This is the common form of greeting in the writings of Paul. It is not found earlier than Paul and it is probable that he formed this combination of Greek and Hebrew greeting as a Christian form of greeting. However, F. F. Bruce suggests that the formula "grace and peace" is a variant on "mercy and peace" which was current in Jewish circles (See his Commentary in the *Word Biblical Commentary,* 8).

The normal Greek letter would begin with "greeting" (Greek: *chairo*) which is from the same root as Paul's word "grace" (Greek: *charis*). Here the word "grace" fundamentally refers to "all the blessings which God bestows through Christ." "Peace" (Greek: *eirene*) is the normal Hebrew form of greeting which indicates something like "I pray that you may prosper." It is about the same as the Hebrew *shalom.* To the words "Grace to you and peace" Paul normally adds the phrase "from

God our Father, and the Lord Jesus Christ" as is found in the King James Version. The addition of these words does not change the meaning of Paul's statement and on the basis of the best textual evidence they should be omitted here. If they are accepted, this is another instance of joining "God the Father" and "the Lord Jesus Christ" under one preposition to emphasize the deity of Christ.

II. REVIEW OF THE HISTORY OF
THE THESSALONIAN CHURCH, 1:2-10

A. Their faithfulness, 1:2-3

V:2 We give thanks to God always for you all, making mention of you in our prayers; V:3 remembering without ceasing your work of faith and labor of love and patience of hope in our Lord Jesus Christ, before our God and Father;

V:2 We give thanks to God always—Almost invariably Paul has some form of thanksgiving near the beginning of his epistles as he does here. When Timothy arrived with news about the Christians in Thessalonica, Paul was grateful for the faith being demonstrated in their lives and he expressed thanks to God for them. The use of the plural "we give thanks" shows that Silvanus and Timothy shared the feeling of gratitude. The use of the present tense verb for "thanks" and the adverb "always" emphasize the constancy of the thanksgiving.

for you all,—These words indicate that Paul and his co-workers remembered the individual Christians in Thessalonica. Paul uses similar words in Ephesians 1:16 and Philippians 1:8. Of course, Paul was aware of the imperfections among these Christians (cf. 3:10), but they had made great strides toward the goal of spiritual maturity considering the time involved.

making mention of you in our prayers;—This is the first of three participle phrases that elaborate on the thanksgiving. This one is a circumstantial participle telling how the thanksgiving was offered to God. Thanksgiving was expressed in prayer. There is an emphasis on prayer in all of Paul's writings.

V:3 remembering without ceasing—This is the second of the circumstantial participles relating to thanksgiving. This one tells when the thanksgiving was offered to God. The present tense participle, "remembering, indicates continuous action and that idea is further emphasized by the adverb translated "without ceasing." This does not indicate that Paul and his colleagues remembered nothing but the Thessalonians, but it emphasizes the strong interest they maintained in these new converts.

your work of faith—The meaning is that they had accepted Jesus as the Christ and Savior, had put their trust in Him and that faith had motivated them to work. The same grammatical construction is found in Romans 1:5 and 16:26. Paul preached with the intent that faith would be the outcome and that faith would motivate obedience. The word "work" is a subjective genitive which means that it refers to that which springs from faith.

and labor of love—The order is clear: first faith, then love. Love does not replace faith but demonstrates it. "Labor" (Greek: *kopos*) means "fatiguing toil, intense labor united with trouble." The concern for the object of love does not stop with ordinary effort, but goes the second mile for the benefit of the other person. Only love can account for the voluntary labor spoken of here. Our love is a reflection of God's prior love to us (cf. 1 John 4:10).

and patience of hope—Patience, or stedfastness, is the third visible aspect of the Thessalonian Christians which brought about the thanksgiving (vs. 2). Patience (Greek: *hupomone*) is not a quiet, passive resignation to fate, but it is an active, courageous quality of life even in the face of tremendous difficulties. The patience of these Christians sprang from their hope. Hope is more than desire, it is filled with expectation, even certainty. Hope is clearly related to faith and love here, but it was the mark which most clearly distinguished between the Christian and the pagan. The pagan had little to look forward to: the speculation about the immortality of the soul for himself, and the possibility of an eternally recurring cycle of history. The Christian looked to Jesus Christ who had already overcome death and was to come again for His people. As mentioned above, faith, love and hope are listed in the proper order. Faith looks back to what God has done; love is a response to a living Savior and hope looks to His coming again.

in our Lord Jesus Christ,—Some take this phrase as referring to the whole of the preceding, including the work of faith and labor of love (Neil). If it is taken in that way, it means that the whole of the Christian life is in Christ. That is true but the context seems to limit this phrase to hope which is in Christ. It should be taken as an objective genitive and may be translated more literally as "patience of hope of our Lord Jesus Christ." Since the larger context continually refers to the coming of Christ at the end of time, it is the Lord Himself who is the object of hope.

before our God and Father;—The exact connection of this phrase is disputed. Some make it connect with the word "remembering" at the beginning of verse three. The translators of the 20th Century New Testament, the Revised Standard Version, the New English Bible and Good News for Modern Man adopt this possibility as do several commentaries.

The main difficulty with that connection is the great distance between "remembering" and this phrase. It is more natural to connect these words with the phrase immediately before it. That makes the words apply to the readers rather than to the writers. Assuming this connection, do these words connect with all three elements of their Christian lives just mentioned, or only to the last one? Since the previous phrase "in our Lord Jesus Christ" is best limited to the words "patience of hope," then this one should also be limited to the same words. The meaning, then, is that their hope is centered in the Lord Jesus Christ whose coming they eagerly await, but that hope is theirs only because they stand before God as His children. They live now with a sense of His presence, but look to the time when they will stand before Him face to face. That will be the fulfillment of their hope, the completion of their salvation.

B. Their reception of the gospel exemplary, 1:4-7

V:4 knowing, brethren beloved of God, your election, V:5 how that our gospel came not unto you in word only, but also in power, and in the Holy Spirit, and in much assurance: even as ye know what manner of men we showed ourselves toward you for your sake. V:6 And ye became imitators of us, and of the Lord, having received the word in much affliction, with joy of the Holy Spirit; V:7 so that ye became an ensample to all that believe in Macedonia and in Achaia.

V:4 knowing, brethren beloved of God,—This participle phrase also refers back to the subject of the main verb "we give thanks" in verse 2 and presents the reason for the thanksgiving. The word translated "knowing" is from *oida* which implies that the knowledge came not by revelation, nor by intuition, but from observation. The remainder of the chapter tells what led the missionaries to conclude that the readers were among God's elect.

The word "brethren" is a common term in Paul's writings. It is used fourteen times in 1 Thessalonians. It accents the strong attachment of the writers to the people of Thessalonica. These readers are a part of the spiritual brotherhood into which all genuine followers of Jesus Christ are inducted (cf. Acts 2:47). The word "brethren" is intensified by the addition of "beloved of God." This exact phrase is used only here in the New Testament although a near equivalent is found in 2 Thessalonians 2:13. In this verse the emphasis is on the active exercise of God's love toward the people. The use of the perfect tense shows that they were already in a state of having been loved and were continuing in that state.

your election,—The noun "election" (Greek: *ekloge*) is always used in the New Testament of divine action. In this verse it is the election, or choice, of the Thessalonians to be a part of God's covenant people which is the ground for the thanksgiving. Such a statement would be especially meaningful to a group of people composed largely of Gentiles. In the past the Jews had been God's chosen people, but now, in the Christian age, any person of any race who accepts the gospel call is among the elect (cf. Acts 10:34,35; 2 Thessalonians 2:13,14). God's election of people always involves two things: (1) God's revelation of His love, and (2) man's willingness to respond to God's gracious offer in His own way. These points are made clear in the following verses.

V:5 how that our gospel came not unto you in word only,— The writers now give the reasons underlying their knowledge that the Christians of Thessalonica were of the elect. The conjunction "how" (Greek: *hoti*) introduces an explanation. The writers first speak of their own experience. They had preached the gospel in Thessalonica (Acts 17:1ff.). The use of the word "gospel" shows that the content of the preaching was good news of God's action in and through Jesus Christ. The fact that this gospel "came" to them indicates that it did not originate with the preachers but with God. The phrase "our gospel" means that the preachers had made it their own and that they had been entrusted to preach it. The gospel did not come to Thessalonica "in word only." It did come in word, that is, in human speech, but there was more than mere words involved. The gospel cannot be preached without words.

but also in power,—This phrase evidently does not refer to miraculous power since no miracle is mentioned in the account of the first preaching in Thessalonica. The statement as found here points to the power of God which is in the gospel (Romans 1:16), and the preachers were aware of divine help. Whenever the gospel is proclaimed, God is present and at work.

and in the Holy Spirit,—These words make two points in light of other Scriptures: (1) the preachers were guided by the Holy Spirit in their preaching, and (2) the Holy Spirit working through the preached word convicted the people of sin and led to conversion (cf. John 16:8-13; Ephesians 6:17). It should be noted that the absence of the definite article "the" in the Greek text before the words Holy Spirit does not mean that the Spirit Himself is not meant.

and in much assurance;—The preachers had perfect assurance that their message was true and powerful. Such certainty on the part of Paul and his associates was a part of the way they came to know of the election of the readers.

They had no doubt as to the reality of the election and neither did the Thessalonians. The work of preaching the gospel is to do service to God and to the hearers. It seems a necessity for the preacher to have full confidence in the message. **even as ye know what manner of men we showed ourselves toward you for your sake.**—The disciples in Thessalonica knew what type persons the missionaries were while among them. There was no indication of self-seeking, but there was an obvious interest in the well-being of the Thessalonians. In this epistle, an appeal is made to the knowledge of the readers several times (cf. 1:5; 2:1,2,5,11; 3:3,4; 4:2). The following verse shows how the gospel had affected the Thessalonians.

V:6 And ye became imitators of us, and of the Lord,—The word "and" shows that additional evidence about their election is being presented. The word "ye" is in an emphatic position and marks the change of subject from the missionaries to the readers. There had been an obvious and dramatic change in the lives of the converts, and now it is to that external demonstration of the change that attention is given. The change was demonstrated by the fact that they "became imitators" of the preachers. The word "imitators" involves more than merely being followers as the KJV indicates. Rather, as they observed the life of the missionaries they were moved to act like them. At the same time they became imitators of the Lord because Paul and his co-workers were imitators of Christ (cf. 1 Corinthians 11:1).

having received the word in much affliction,—Spiritual growth came only after these converts had received the message preached by the missionaries. The word translated "received" is used elsewhere in the New Testament with the sense of a hospitable reception, a welcome (John 4:45; Luke 10:8; Hebrews 11:31). Even after their conversion, their response to the Word was just as enthusiastic even though it involved "much affliction." "Affliction" (Greek: *thlipsis*) is mentioned often in both Thessalonian epistles (1 Thessalonians 1:6; 3:3,7; 2 Thessalonians 1:4,6) because opposition to the message was present from the beginning (Acts 17:5-9) and grew into bitter opposition (2 Thessalonians

2:14-16). At first, the defiance was aimed only at the missionaries, it seems, but soon spread to the converts. The word "affliction" refers to pressure of hostile opposition and persecution from without. Such pressure came from Jews (Acts 17:5) and evidently from pagans (1 Thessalonians 2:13).

with joy of the Holy Spirit;—The preposition "with" (Greek: *meta*) followed by the genitive case indicates that joy was being experienced along with the affliction. Such a combination as joy accompanied by pain is not a natural thing. The source of it is noted here as "the Holy Spirit." The same relationship of joy and affliction is seen in Acts 5:41 when the disciples were "rejoicing that they were counted worthy to suffer dishonor for the Name" and in the ability of Paul and Silas to pray and sing hymns to God after being beaten and imprisoned (Acts 16:25). The point seems to be that when they received the Spirit inspired word, they were filled with joy which more than compensated for the afflictions brought by the persecutors (cf. Romans 8:18).

V:7 so that ye became an ensample to all that believe in Macedonia and in Achaia.—"So that ye became" points to a definite result of the things stated in verse 6. The use of the plural "ye" points to the individual members of the Thessalonian church as the source of this effect. The word "ensample" is from the Greek word *tupos* and here is the same as the more modern word "example" or "pattern." Those who began as imitators have become the example for others to imitate. These Christians had become an example "to all that believe." They may also have been an example to unbelievers, but the text points to other Christians outside Thessalonica, namely "in Macedonia and Achaia." The example was evidently not in the reception of the message but in the suffering for it. Notice also that the word translated "that believe" is a present tense participle form and indicates those who had an abiding faith.

Macedonia and Achaia were two Roman provinces which made up what was ancient Greece. Thessalonica was located in Macedonia and was the provincial capital of the northern area, and Corinth was the capital of Achaia, the southern province, where 1 Thessalonians was written. That the writers were thinking of the two distinct provinces is clear from the repetition of the preposition "in" (Greek: *en*) with the definite article before each name. At the time of writing, Christianity was established only in the main centers, but it was spreading through all parts of the two provinces.

C. They had been active in sounding out the word, 1:8-10

V:8 For from you hath sounded forth the word of the Lord, not only in Macedonia and Achaia, but in every place your faith to God-ward is gone forth; so that we need not to speak anything. V:9 For they themselves report concerning us what manner of entering in we had unto you; and how ye turned unto God from idols, to serve a living and true God, V:10 and to wait for his Son from heaven, whom he raised from the dead, even Jesus, who delivereth us from the wrath to come.

V:8 For from you hath sounded forth the word of the Lord,— These words are given as evidence for the statement in verse 7. There is an emphasis on the words "from you" indicating that the action of the verb came from them as the starting point. The verb "hath sounded forth" (Greek: *execheo*) is found only here in the New Testament. It is a vivid word and indicates a loud resounding noise such as a trumpet or thunder. The word is in the perfect tense which denotes the continuing activity or, perhaps more to the point here, the persistence of the proclamation. That which is "sounded forth" is "the word of the Lord." The exact phrase is used only here and in 2 Thessalonians 3:1 in Paul's writings but there are similar expressions. This phrase is used in Acts and is a standard phrase in the Old Testament to describe a prophet's words as he makes known God's will. "Of the Lord" is a subjective genitive meaning "the word which comes from the Lord."

not only in Macedonia and Achaia, but in every place your faith to God-ward is gone forth;— In verse 7 Macedonia and Achaia both have the definite article and are considered as two specific areas, but in verse 8 they are linked under one article and are to be considered as one area, namely Greece. This area is contrasted with "in every place." Since Thessalonica was an important seaport serving ships from many places and located on the Egnatian Way, a much traveled road, it is not surprising that Paul and his friends knew of the faith of these Christians. It is very likely that the charges against the Christians in that city (Acts 17:6,7) had been reported to Rome and would have been talked about there. Aquila and his wife Priscilla had recently arrived in Corinth from Rome and had doubtless brought news of such talk. There is, therefore, a sound basis for the statement about their faith. The use of the perfect tense verb "has gone forth" (Greek: *exeleluthen*) indicates that reports of their faith have gone out and continue to go out at the time of writing. Their faith was "toward God." The use of the preposition "toward" (Greek: *pros*) indicates that their faith was directed toward and had as its object "the God," the one true God whom they now know and serve. Such faith is needed today.

so that we need not to speak anything,—The reference here is not to the gospel, it needed to be preached. The faith of the Thessalonians was already known among the people where the missionaries journeyed. When word of their faith had already been spread, there was no need to speak of it anymore.

V:9 For they themselves report concerning us what manner of entering in we had unto you;—Instead of Paul and his co-workers telling what had happened in Thessalonica, others were continuing to report what had happened in that city. The report being heard had two parts. First, they spoke of the "manner of entering" the city. This combination of words evidently refers to the reception given the preachers when they arrived (cf. 1:5) and includes their entire stay. The words "unto you" (Greek: *pros humas*) indicate that their ministry was done in a person to person relationship. The missionaries were open and above-board in dealing with the people.

and how ye turned unto God from idols,—This is the second part of the report about what had happened in Thessalonica. The people had "turned unto God." The word "turned" (Greek:

epistrepho) is here in the aorist tense which implies a change immediately consequent upon a deliberate choice. It is the normal word for conversion to Christianity (Acts 14:15; 9:35; 11:21; 15:19; 26:18). The word is not characteristic in Paul's writing being used only here and in 2 Corinthians 3:16 where it is a quote from the Old Testament, and in Galatians 4:9 where it refers to the danger of turning back from the faith of the gospel. The Thessalonian Christians had made a definite change "toward" or "unto (Greek: *pros*) God from idols." The Greek text has a definite article "the" with the word "Idols" which makes it clear that it refers to all the idols they had known in the past. "Idols" is from a word (Greek: *eidolon*) which may be used for both the images worshipped by pagans and also of the false gods represented by the images. It also conveys the suggestion that the pagan gods are no more real than their images. The preposition used means "from" or "away from" (Greek: *apo*) and shows a definite turning from the idols so that they are now separated from any idol worship.

Some have suggested that there is a problem between this verse and the account in Acts 17:4 which mentions preaching in the synagogue only. That would mean that only Jews heard the message and they were not idol worshippers. In response, it is said that these words refer to God-fearers whom Paul and his colleagues had confronted in the synagogue [A. J. Hultgen, *Paul's Gospel and Mission: The Outlook from His Letter to the Romans* (Philadelphia: Fortress Press, 1985), 140-42]. God-fearers are evidently meant by the phrase "devout Greeks" in Acts 17:4, but such had most likely already broken with idol worship. Some may not have completely broken all old ties, but it is doubtful if the words in 1 Thessalonians refer to that group. It seems more likely that there was a period of preaching outside the synagogue even though it is not mentioned in Acts [See the Introduction].

to serve a living and true God,—This is the first of two purpose clauses. The words "to serve" are from a verb form which basically means "to serve as a slave," and emphasizes the completeness of the surrender to God. Such service as indicated speaks of absolute devotion and recognition of His rightful Lordship over mankind. The absence of the definite article "before God" draws attention to His character which is the very opposite of the idols they formerly served. The phrase in our English translation "a God" does not leave open the possibility of the existence of other gods as the adjectives describing God show. The One to whom the Thessalonians have turned is "living," a word that does not mean simply that He is alive or that He exists, but it means that He is active. Living, in the Bible, means something vibrant and dynamic. To speak of God as "living" is to make the claim that He is actively present and a force to be reckoned with (cf. Acts 14:14; 17:24-28). This God is also described as "true," a word that means "genuine, true, real." It is used to contrast this God with pagan gods who are thought of as counterfeit, or as having no objective existence.

V:10 and to wait for his Son from heaven,—The second purpose statement is that they now have an attitude of expectancy of Jesus Christ's return. The word translated "to wait for" is found only here in the New Testament. It means "to await one whose coming is expected." It also includes the idea of patience and confidence according to George Abbott-Smith's Lexicon. The use of the present tense implies that this was to be their continuing attitude. The Thessalonian epistles give the coming of Christ a prominent place. The return is "from (literally "out of") heaven" (literally "the heavens"). The use of the plural indicates Semitic usage and should not raise speculations about the number of heavens. The point is that Christ is now, at the time of writing and still, at the right hand of God and it is from the presence of God that He will come. "Son" is applied to Christ only here in these epistles.

whom he raised from the dead, even Jesus,—This clause is decisive evidence of Jesus' Sonship, as in Romans 1:4. The resurrection is mentioned as a guarantee of His coming again at the general resurrection and at the Judgment. These words are a clear historical reference to Jesus' resurrection which was the central event of the early preaching to both Jews (Acts

2:24-32; 3:15; 4:10; 13:30) and to Gentiles (Acts 17:31). Obviously it had been emphasized in Thessalonica also. To Jews it showed that Jesus was the Old Testament Messiah and to Gentiles it demonstrated the power of God which was given to the raised and glorified Savior in His present position. The mention of the name Jesus underscores the identity of the risen and coming Lord with Jesus of Nazareth.

who delivereth us from the wrath to come.—Jesus is further described in these words. The present participle with the definite article translated "who delivereth" indicates that Jesus is permanently our Deliverer. He delivers us from evil each day (Matthew 6:13) and will complete the deliverance at the end of time. The "wrath to come" beyond doubt refers to the wrath of God. It is being revealed even now (Romans 1:18), and apart from the gospel of Jesus Christ there is no way of escaping it. Of course the wrath of God is His personal, necessary reaction against sin but it is never malicious or, in a bad sense, emotional. During this age deliverance is available on a continuing basis but it is all leading to the deliverance carried out once for all at the end of this world system (cf. 1 Thessalonians 5:9; Romans 2:5-11).

Chapter 2

III. THE RELATIONSHIP OF THE WRITERS TO THE CHURCH, 2:1-3:13

The beginning of chapter 2 is the transition point from the opening statement to the body of the epistle. The section continues to 3:13. There is an obvious change of tone in 2:1-12 where the writers begin a defense. These preachers had arrived in Thessalonica fresh from ill-treatment and insult, but they boldly proclaimed the message of Christ in this area. They did not deceive or flatter, they did not seek personal advantage or gain. They even earned their own living and their lives would bear close examination.

A. The Proper Motive in Preaching, 2:1-4

V:1 For yourselves, brethren, know our entering in unto you, that it hath not been found vain: V:2 but having suffered before and been shamefully treated, as ye know, at Philippi, we waxed bold in our God to speak unto you the gospel of God in much conflict. V:3 For our exhortation is not of error, nor of uncleanness, nor in guile: V:4 but even as we have been approved of God to be intrusted with the gospel, so we speak; not as pleasing men, but God who proveth our hearts.

V:1 For yourselves, brethren, know our entering in unto you,— This verse is clearly an introduction to a defense. The context shows clearly that Paul and his co-workers had been accused of having some ulterior motive in their work. The opposition was trying to destroy the faith of these new Christians by undermining their confidence in the preachers. If those preachers were religious charlatans and were only interested in gaining personal honor or financial gain, the faith of the people would be shaken and perhaps lost.

Having explained fully the reasons for the thanksgiving (1:2-10), the main reason for the epistle is presented. The word "for" (Greek: *gar*) refers to the stream of thought in the previous verses. Wherever the missionaries traveled, people were bearing witness to their work and its results in Thessalonica. Those people were reporting what they had heard, and possibly seen, but the Thessalonian Christians knew by personal experience what had happened (cf. 1:4,5). Note the emphatic use of the word "yourselves" in contrast to "themselves" in 1:9.

that it hath not been found vain:—"That" is from *hoti*, a causal conjunction which explains and expands the previous clause. The precise meaning of the rest of this clause is difficult and depends upon the meaning of the word translated "vain" (Greek: *kene*). Some view the word as referring to the results of the ministry in Thessalonica (e.g. D. Lipscomb, *Gospel Advocate Commentary;* J. Moffatt, *The Expositor's Greek Testament;* New English Bible). Others, like Milligan and J. B. Lightfoot, think the word refers to the character of the preaching. Raymond Kelcy, however, points out that it was the "visit" or "entering" that was "not in vain" (Sweet Commentary Series). That point, plus the fact that the basic meaning of *kene* is "empty," shows that the statement affirms the earnestness and purposefulness of the visit. These men came not to get, but to give the greatest treasure available, the gospel of Jesus Christ. The use of the perfect tense verb to express the idea shows the action as accomplished and as a settled fact.

V:2 but having suffered before and been shamefully treated, as ye know, at Philippi,—The use of the strong conjunction "but" (Greek: *alla*) emphasizes the sharp contrast with the charges implied in verse 1. Far from being "vain," their work was done with confidence and courage. The Christians addressed knew about the experiences of the missionaries at Philippi before they arrived in Thessalonica (cf. Acts 16:16-40). The words "having suffered" indicate physical suffering, probably referring to the beating received, and the words "shamefully treated" refer to insult and/or mental distress when they were stripped and beaten without proper examination of the charges against them, especially since they were Roman citizens. These past experiences did not keep the missionaries from boldly proclaiming the gospel message even with the prospect of suffering similar treatment. The words "as ye know" show the desire to keep the readers thinking back to the time of the event.

we waxed bold in our God to speak unto you the gospel of God in much conflict.—"We waxed bold" is from a word that involves the meanings of "boldness" and "confidence" (Greek: *parresiazomai*). Every time this word is used in the New Testament it has to do with preaching the gospel. The "boldness" or "confidence" was "in God." Shortly before writing these words, Paul had been "in weakness, and in fear, and in much trembling" (1 Corinthians 2:3). Such a state of mind passed with the coming of Silas and Timothy from Macedonia (Acts 18:5) bringing good news about the recent converts in Thessalonica. The boldness here is based on a new surge of confidence in God's work.

"To speak unto you" explains what the boldness and confidence motivated the preachers to do. "The gospel of God" refers to the message of which God Himself was author and revealer. The preaching was "in much conflict." The word "conflict" (Greek: *agon*) indicates "to engage in intense struggle, involving physical or nonphysical force against strong opposition—'to struggle, to fight'" (Louw & Nida, *Greek-English Lexicon*, 39:29). Acts 17:5-9 is a good commentary on this statement. Note that the English word "agony" comes from this Greek word. It seems a waste of time and effort to debate whether "conflict" refers to inner struggle or external pressures. No doubt both were experienced by these preachers.

V:3 For our exhortation—By using the explanatory "for," (Greek: *gar*) the writers proceed to establish further the sincerity of their motives in preaching. Three emphatic denials are given regarding the preaching. The noun "exhortation" has several possible meanings: "a calling to one's aid, summons; an appeal, exhortation, encouragement; comfort." The precise meaning must be determined from the context. In this verse "appeal" or "exhortation" is best because the word describes the preaching with its quest for a favorable response.

is not of error,—The verb "is" is added for proper English. The preposition "of" (Greek: *ek*) literally means "out of" or "out from within." The thought is that the preaching of the gospel of God did not originate out of error. Error is more than an innocent mistake. The word implies "a wandering from the path of truth, a voluntary giving in to that which leads astray and is therefore sinful." The claim is that these preachers knew what is truth and had no intention of misleading others.

nor of uncleanness,—Second, the "exhortation" did not spring from "uncleanness." "Uncleanness" (Greek: *akatharsia*) is often used in the New Testament to refer to sexual impurity (e.g., 4:7; Romans 1:24; Galatians 5:19; Colossians 3:5) and some may have accused Paul and his co-workers of some type of religious prostitution such as was characteristic of many cults of the day. It is certain that Christians were openly charged with immorality later. Others think that the word here must refer to a "lack of integrity," or "moral foulness, dirty ways, of any sort," or "impure motives." It seems best to take the word in its widest application and allow it to deny any charge that would mark the preachers as having impure motives in their work.

nor in guile:—The word "guile" (Greek: *dolos*) basically means "to deceive by using trickery and falsehood." The change of preposition from "of" with both error and uncleanness to "in" with guile changes the attention from source to atmosphere. The words deny that the exhortation

29

had used any such manipulative methods to ensnare converts. The preachers had been open and straightforward in their work.

V:4 but even as we have been approved of God to be intrusted with the gospel, so we speak;—The true state of these preachers was one of openness and honesty which resulted in God's approval of them to proclaim His gospel. "We have been approved" is from a verb which indicates that approval came only after testing. The perfect tense indicates that the testing and approval had been completed in the past but that both have continuing results. "Of God" shows that it was God Himself who approved these men and then "entrusted" them "with the gospel." Paul always remembered that his task of preaching was a "stewardship entrusted" to him (cf. 1 Corinthians 9:17; Galatians 1:11,12; 2:7; Acts 20:24; Romans 1:1,5; 1 Timothy 1:11; Titus 1:3).

The words "so we speak" are the principle statement of this verse. This shows the obedient response to the task given them. "So" shows that they preached under the consciousness that they were tested, approved and commissioned. "We speak" is from a present tense verb indicating that it was their normal practice to speak the gospel to others.

not as pleasing men,—Paul and his colleagues emphatically deny any thought of shaping their message for the purpose of "pleasing men." It is true that the apostle did say that he pleased "all men in all things, not seeking mine own profit, but the profit of the many, that they may be saved" (1 Corinthians 10:33). The context of the two statements is very different, however.

but God who proveth our hearts.—The conjunction "but" (Greek: *alla*) is a strong one and it emphasizes the fact that their concern is to please God only. The God whom these missionaries desire to please is the one who continues to test and approve their hearts. The word "heart" as used here refers to the whole of one's inner life including his thoughts, will and emotions. Nothing in their lives was hidden from God as the plural "our" shows.

B. The proper conduct in daily living, 2:5-12

V:5 For neither at any time were we found using words of flattery, as ye know, nor a cloak of covetousness, God is witness; V:6 nor seeking glory of men, neither from you nor from others, when we might have claimed authority as apostles of Christ. V:7 But we were gentle in the midst of you, as when a nurse cherisheth her own children: V:8 even so, being affectionately desirous of you, we were well pleased to impart unto you, not the gospel of God only, but also our own souls, because ye were become very dear to us. V:9 For ye remember, brethren, our labor and travail: working night and day, that we might not burden any of you, we preached unto you the gospel of God. V:10 Ye are witnesses, and God also, how holily and righteously and unblameably we behaved ourselves toward you that believe: V:11 as ye know how we dealt with each one of you, as a father with his own children, exhorting you, and encouraging you, and testifying, V:12 to the end that ye should walk worthily of God, who calleth you into his own kingdom and glory.

V:5 For neither at any time were we found using words of flattery,—The conjunction "for" (Greek: *gar*) resumes the explanation which was introduced by the same word in verse 3. As in that verse, there are three separate, but specific, charges denied. These preachers had at no time been guilty of the charges mentioned. The translation "were we found using" is subject to misunderstanding. The words do not suggest that they "were found out" since there is no suggestion of concealment. The statement is simply that they did not at any time use flattery. "Flattery" (Greek: *kolakeia*) refers to the use of "praise as a means of gratifying someone's vanity" and it includes the idea of gaining one's own ends. The use of such speech seems to have been common in the first century world, but was not used by Paul and his co-workers.

as ye know,—This is the third appeal to the reader's knowledge of the work of the preachers while they were in Thessalonica (2:,2,3,5). The words serve as an appeal for the readers to verify the truthfulness of the statement just made, and perhaps to the following.

nor a cloak of covetousness,—This second denial rejects the charge that the missionaries were motivated by disguised greed. The word "cloak" (Greek: *prophasis*) means a "falsely alleged motive, pretext, ostensible reason, excuse" and is evidently used here to refer to a pretext used to conceal the reality "of covetousness." "Covetousness" (Greek: *pleonexia*) is translated "greed" in some versions (cf. RSV, NEB, NIV). The basic meaning is a "desire to have more," but of that to which one has no right. Paul uses this same word in Colossians 3:5 where he defines it as "idolatry" primarily because it is totally self-centered. These missionaries have never at any time been motivated by selfishness.

God is witness;—First, the readers are called as witnesses, now God is called upon to witness. The defense offered is very serious in tone and comes from deep conviction that none of the charges will stand under close investigation.

V:6 nor seeking glory of men, neither from you nor from others,—The third denial concerns charges of seeking glory or praise from men. Paul elsewhere shows that the glory is in the message preached, not in himself (cf. 1 Corinthians 2:2; 2 Corinthians 4:5; 3:4-11). The same attitude is present here. The word "seeking" is given emphasis in this statement. The word (Greek: *zeteo*) means "to seek in order to find," thus to search for something diligently and earnestly. The negative "nor" (Greek: *oute*) shows that no such seeking to find glory from men was in these preachers. "Glory" (Greek: *doxa*) is translated "praise" in the NIV and "honor" in the NEB. The word literally means "brightness," "splendor," or "radiance," and here carries the idea of "fame," or "honor." The fact is, at Thessalonica Jason and other Christians were exposed to great danger along with the preachers as the readers knew. The denial of such seeking includes not only the work at Thessalonica but wherever they had been. The claim that "glory" here refers to monetary gain is very doubtful.

when we might have claimed authority as apostles of Christ.—Although the best Greek text begins verse 7 here, the grammar shows that this clause goes with, and completes, verse 6. The first word is a participle and is best taken as a concessive, "although we might have." It qualifies the fact just stated, although the preachers have not sought honor from men, they did have a right to make some such claim. The expression translated "claimed authority" may literally be "to be in weight." The noun used is *baros* and means "weight" or "burden," but the context indicates that it refers to the missionaries' right of, or authority to claim, financial support for their work. Paul often uses words related to this one in regard to his right to receive support (e.g., verse 9; 2 Thessalonians 3:8; 2 Corinthians 11:9; 12:16). He also makes it clear that the right to support may be given up (1 Corinthians 9:6-10,12). There were most likely several reasons for giving up the right to be supported. Perhaps it was the rabbinical training which forbade making religious teaching a means of livelihood (*Pirqe 'Abot* 1:13; 4:7), or Paul's independent spirit (Acts 20:33,34), or the desire to set a good example (2 Thessalonians 3:9; 1 Corinthians 9:12). The latter seems to be the basis for the KJV translating "when we might have been burdensome."

Another view of the words translated "claimed authority" deserves mention. The immediate context refers to receiving personal glory, that is, some outward honor or distinction. The meaning would then refer to their right to claim some personal importance, or to an assertion of their weight of power and influence. The NASB reflects this thought: "we might have asserted our authority." It is possible that the words are intended to convey both ideas, but the primary emphasis seems to be on the right to claim support.

The phrase "as apostles of Christ" gives the basis for the claim mentioned above. Timothy and Silvanus are placed in the category of apostles. Evidently the word "apostle" is used in a nontechnical sense and is not intended to call them apostles in the same sense as the twelve and Paul (cf. Acts 1:21,22; 1 Corinthians 9:1,2; Galatians 1:11,12; 2:7-9). Others are called apostles in the New Testament who were given the task of preaching the word, and of some who had been sent by the church for a specific mission. Here the word seems to mean that these men were in Thessalonica as preachers of the gospel of Christ.

V:7 But we were gentle in the midst of you, as when a nurse cherisheth her own children:—"But" (Greek: *alla*) refers to the positive side of the missionaries conduct in Thessalonica and emphasizes the contrast with the negative charges. The variant reading, "babes," has good manuscript evidence but it seems inappropriate in the context. In the next clause the writers compare themselves to a nurse or mother caring for her own children. Also the word "gentle" provides a proper contrast to being a burden in verse 6. The phrase "her own children" (Greek: *ta heautes tekna*) indicates that the word "nurse" (Greek: *trophos*) refers to a nursing mother (Louw & Nida, *Greek-English Lexicon*). The word translated "cherisheth" (Greek: *thalpo*) means "to keep warm," or "to cherish with tender love" and emphasizes deep concern for the readers.

V:8 even so, being affectionately desirous of you,—"Even so" refers to the thought of verse 7, but reemphasizes the thought by dropping the figure and stating explicitly how their conduct was expressed. "Being affectionately desirous" (Greek: *homeiromai*) comes from a rare word used only here in the New Testament, but the meaning is clear. The preachers continued to have a constant "yearning for" the readers even after being separated from them for a time.

we were well pleased to impart unto you, not the gospel of God only, but also our own souls, because you were become very dear to us.—The deep concern so moved the missionaries that they were continually pleased to share their whole being with the Thessalonians. The wording indicates what actually happened rather than what was contemplated. The words "to impart" (Greek: *metadidomi*) literally mean "to share a thing with anyone." These preachers gave not merely words, but their very souls, i.e., all that they were, even to putting their lives in danger. This is clearly the language of love rather than of selfishness. The deep-seated love was because the readers had become "beloved" or "very dear" (Greek: *agapetoi*) to the writers. The verse closes, as it began, with a reference to the strong feelings the missionaries held toward the readers.

V:9 For ye remember, brethren, our labor and travail:—"For" (Greek: *gar*) introduces further evidence for what has already been said about the work among the Thessalonian Christians. Once again an appeal is made to the memory of the people to substantiate what is said. The word "labor" (Greek: *kopos*) is defined at 1:3. The word "travail" (Greek: *mochthos*) emphasizes the toil or painfulness of the work. These words are used together in 2 Thessalonians 3:8 and 2 Corinthians 11:27 with the same basic meaning. The phrase may be translated "our toil and trouble."

working night and day,—"Working" (Greek: *ergazomai*) marks the circumstances attending the preaching. Possibly the meaning is that they worked as they preached. Both "night" and "day" are in the genitive case and are genitives of time, therefore, the phrase means that the missionaries worked during the night and during the day, not continuously throughout the twenty-four hour period. In Thessalonica, then, as later in Corinth (1 Corinthians 4:12) and Ephesus (Acts 19:12), Paul supported himself by manual labor, and his co-workers did the same.

that we might not burden any of you,—This is a purpose statement making it clear that these men worked diligently to avoid laying the "burden" (Greek: *epibareo*) of support on the Thessalonians.

we preached unto you the gospel of God.—"We preached" (Greek: *kerusso*) is a common expression in the New Testament for preaching the gospel (cf. Mark 1:14; 1 Corinthians 1:23; 9:27). "The gospel of God" is the same as above in verses 2 and 8.

This is one place where some critics have questioned Paul's honesty. From Philippians 4:15,16, we learn that the Philippian Christians had sent financial help to him. Why does he not mention that fact here if he is completely honest? There are several possible reasons why the outside help is not mentioned. It is possible that the support from Philippi was not adequate to supply the needs of the three preachers. It may be that it is not mentioned in order to avoid any embarrassment to the Thessalonians since the help came from another congregation. It seems more likely that Paul is simply following his normal practice of refusing support from the people where he was preaching at the time. He did not want to be a burden to them nor did he want to leave any grounds for criticism of his motives.

V:10 Ye are witnesses, and God also,— Once again the writers show great confidence in the Christians in Thessalonica. A similar appeal is in verse 5 of this chapter. Here the witness (Greek: *martus*) of the converts and that of God are closely related, no doubt for emphasis. The tone of this verse strongly suggests that it is in response to real accusations made by opponents of the church with the purpose of defaming the character of the preachers and thus their message hoping to turn the converts against them.

how holily and righteously and unblamably—The word "how" (Greek: *hos*) is an adverb expressing manner. The readers and God can testify to the manner of life exhibited by the preachers. The word is followed by three additional adverbs: "holily" (Greek: *hosios*), "righteously" (Greek: *dikaios*), and "unblamably" (Greek: *amemptos*). J. B. Lightfoot has suggested that "holily" and "righteously" refer to man's duty toward God and man's duty to other men respectively. He bases his thoughts on the use of these words in classical Greek. F. F. Bruce and Leon Morris think that the Greek of the New Testament does not substantiate Lightfoot's view. The word "holily" is used in the New Testament to express an attitude of piety and reverence toward God which would affect one's conduct (Hebrews 7:26; Titus 1:8). "Righteously" is used to describe how man should live before God and men (1 Corinthians 15:34; Titus 2:12). Both these adverbs present a positive statement about the right conduct but the third word, "unblamably," presents a negative statement showing that their conduct did not fall below the proper standard. Note the same word in 1 Thessalonians 5:23 where it is translated "without blame."

we behaved ourselves toward you that believe:—The verb translated "we behaved ourselves" (Greek: *ginomai*)is the same as the one in 2:5,7 and in the second person in 1:6. It has the basic meaning of "becoming" and here implies that the conduct mentioned was not mere chance but the outcome of conscious obedience and effort. The words do not imply that they first came to behave in this way at Thessalonica, but that when they arrived there they soon came to be known as men who lived above reproach. The use of the aorist tense treats the entire stay in Thessalonica as a unit. This exemplary life was recognized by those who believed and they now could serve as witnesses to such conduct.

V:11 As ye know—Here is the fifth appeal in this chapter to the Thessalonian's personal knowledge of the facts about the conduct of the preachers (cf. vss. 1,2,5,9,10).

how we dealt with each one of you,—The clause beginning with "how" (Greek: *hos*) has no finite verb in the original text so the translators of the ASV supply "dealt with" to make good English. Others supply other words or make the participles of the verse function as regular verbs. The meaning is fairly clear in all the major versions regardless of the verb chosen.

The Thessalonians knew about the very personal dealings the missionaries had with them. The word "how" (Greek: *kathaper*) marks an emphatic comparison between events and means "just as," or "precisely as." This word implies the manner as well as the fact and the sense is "you know the way in which we dealt with each one of you." The words "each one of you" puts an emphasis on the individual aspect of the work. The preaching and teaching, whether from house to house or public or both, was designed to meet the questions and needs of each person.

as a father with his own children,—This figure of speech is used by Paul in other epistles where he had been involved in the conversion of the readers (cf. 1 Corinthians 4:14-21; 2 Corinthians 6:13; Galatians 4:19; Philemon 10). Since the time of John Chrysostom, who died about A.D. 407, the figure of a mother nursing her babes has been accepted as showing the tenderness of the apostle's love toward the converts and the figure of a father was used when he speaks of instructing them motivated by the same love.

exhorting you, and encouraging you,—These words are the beginning of verse 12 in the Greek text and in a few translations but that does not in anyway affect the meaning. The two verbs are practically synonymous. "Exhorting" (Greek: *parakaleo*) is the most general word for instruction to converts (1 Thessalonians 3:2,7; 4:1,10,18; 5:11,14) and its frequency in this epistle emphasizes the concern of the preachers that the readers live genuine Christian lives. As used in this verse, the word suggests an urging to pursue some course of conduct. The second verb, "encouraging" (Greek: *paramutheomai*), as used here, seems to mean to "encourage in that course of conduct" just mentioned.

and testifying,—This word (Greek: *marturomai*) is translated "charged" in the KJV and RSV. It has the basic idea of insisting that the readers obey the instructions given.

V:12 to the end that ye should walk worthily of God,—These words are the object of the exhortations presented above. "Walk" (Greek: *peripateo*) is used figuratively here and often in the New Testament to refer to the entire round of life (cf. 1 Corinthians 7:17; Colossians 2:6; 1 Thessalonians 4:1; Romans 6:4). The word "worthily" is an adverb exhorting the readers to conduct themselves in a manner worthy of their relation to God.

who calleth you into his own kingdom and glory.—God, who had called these people to salvation by means of the gospel, 2 Thessalonians 2:13,14 continues to call them to a life of holiness as the present tense participle shows. While in Thessalonica, Paul and his co-workers had preached Jesus as King implying a kingdom (Acts 17:7). The kingdom is both present in the world now (the Christian age) and is to be fully revealed at the end time. Christians have citizenship in heaven (Philippians 3:20) and share in God's glory now, but completely in heaven itself. It is the prospect of the latter that sustains one in the present (cf. Romans 8:18).

C. THE PREACHING WAS THE WORD OF GOD, 2:13-16

V:13 And for this cause we also thank God without ceasing, that, when ye received from us the word of the message, even the word of God, ye accepted it not as the word of men, but, as it is in truth, the word of God, which also worketh in you that believe. V:14 For ye, brethren, became imitators of the churches of God which are in Judaea in Christ Jesus: for ye also suffered the same things of your own countrymen, even as they did of the Jews: V:15 who both killed the Lord Jesus and the prophets, and drove out us, and please not God, and are contrary to all men; V:16 forbidding us to speak to the Gentiles that they may be saved; to fill up their sins always: but the wrath is come upon them to the uttermost.

V:13 And for this cause we also thank God without ceasing,— "And for this cause" may look forward or backward depending on the context. Here it seems to refer to the principle presented in verses 1-4 of this chapter that the gospel is not human but divine. The following words "we also thank God" implies that there had been some news from Thessalonians about their thankfulness for the gospel (cf. 1 Thessalonians 3:6), and now the missionaries are emphasizing their own thankfulness. This view is based on the emphatic use "we" (Greek: *hemeis*) and the word "also" (Greek: *kai*) before the verb. The thanksgiving is offered "without ceasing" as was the remembrance of their work, labor and patience in chapter 1:3.

that, when ye received from us the word of the message,— "That" (Greek: *hoti*) introduces a clause which sets forth the basis for the thanksgiving just mentioned. The temporal participle phrase "when ye received from us" indicates the reception of a message or body of instruction handed down with the intention that it be taught to others (Louw and Nida, *Greek-English Lexicon*, I:27:13). "The word of the message" is literally "a word of hearing," but "hearing" (Greek: *akoe*) here refers to that which is heard, thus the message.

even the word of God,—This phrase emphasizes the divine origin of the message.

ye accepted it—This word (Greek: *dechomai*), in another form, is found in 1:6 where it is translated "having received." See comments there. In this verse there is a real, but slight,

difference between this word and the one translated
"received" (Greek: *paralambano*) in this verse. "Received"
shows that they had given the word a hearing and "accepted"
adds the idea that they had appropriated it to themselves.
**not as the word of men, but, as it is in truth, the word of
God,**—The gospel had been preached by men but had not been
accepted as originating with them but with God. The text
does not state that the converts had merely regarded the
message to be from God, it asserts clearly that it was from
Him.

which also worketh in you that believe.—The word of God
was at work in the readers since their conversion and
continued to work at the writing of this epistle. The use of
the middle voice verb shows that the word bears its life and
power within itself. Elsewhere the word is spoken of as "living
and active" (Hebrews 4:12), it also effects the new birth (1 Peter
1:23), the word builds up and gives an inheritance (Acts 20:32),
and is able to save the soul (James 1:21). Where the word of
God is accepted into one's life as stated here, there it works.
That point is further defined by the use of the appositional
participle phrase, "that believe." The "believing" is an abiding,
continuing belief as indicated by the present tense.

**V:14 For ye, brethren, became imitators of the churches of God
which are in Judaea in Christ Jesus:**—It seems best to take
the connecting word "for" (Greek: *gar*) as confirming the
principle statement of verse 13—their reception of the gospel
as of divine origin. Welcoming the gospel and enduring persecution in some form often go together (cf.
1 Thessalonians 1:6). The reputation of the Thessalonian
Christians as "imitators" was already established as the aorist
passive form of the verb shows (Greek: *egenethete* from
ginomai as in 1:6). They had been imitators of the authors of
the epistle (1:6), but now they are imitators of the churches
"of God" which were located in Judaea. To make it clear that
these churches are Christian, the words "in Christ Jesus" are
added. The churches "in Judaea" are specifically mentioned
because they were particularly the object of Jewish
persecution, and the Jews were the ones who first were

persecuting the Thessalonian Christians (Acts 17:5ff.).

for ye also suffered the same things of your own countrymen, even as they did of the Jews;—The Jewish persecution had aroused the local Gentiles against the Christians. Perhaps some of the family members of the Gentiles were involved in the opposition (Acts 17:4). Word of such events could have been brought by Timothy who had recently arrived from Thessalonica (1 Thessalonians 3:6).

The word "suffered" (Greek: *pascho*) is in the aorist tense and is used to sum up the entire range of suffering instead of one specific event. Both the Judaean churches and the one in Thessalonica had suffered because of their "own countrymen." The word "countrymen" certainly would refer to Gentiles, but does not exclude Jewish people who were local free citizens of Thessalonica (Lightfoot, p. 32). However, the Gentiles seem to be placed at the forefront of the persecution by the phrase "even as they did of the Jews."

V:15 who both killed the Lord Jesus—The mention of the Jews moved the writers to a strong criticism of them. Such harsh language is uncommon in Paul and is no doubt due to the wide scope of the persecution. The leading charge is that they "killed the Lord Jesus." This is the only place in the epistles assigned to Paul that the agents of Jesus' death are specified. It is true that the Roman soldiers actually did the killing (John 19:16ff.; 1 Corinthians 2:8), but the Jews accused Him before Pilate on a fabricated political charge (Luke 23:2) which led to His death. It is interesting that the word translated "killed" (Greek: *apokteino*) has the force of to kill so as "to do away with" or "to eliminate." By separating the words "the Lord" from "Jesus," the writers emphasize that the Lord whom they crucified is in fact the historical Jesus, their fellow Jew according to the flesh (Romans 9:5).

and the prophets,—The killing of the prophets is closely linked to the killing of Jesus. The prophets are Old Testament prophets, the ones who foretold the coming of Jesus as Christ. Essentially the same thought is found in Matthew 23:29-36; Luke 11:47-51; 13:34; Acts 7:52. It is possible that the word "prophets" should be connected with "us" in this passage. The translation would be, "who killed the Lord Jesus, and drove out both the prophets and us." The translation in the ASV is best.

and drove out us,—The verb here is a rare word which implies extreme persecution (Greek: *ekdioko*). The reference is most likely to the recent expulsion of Paul and his friends from Thessalonica (Acts 17:5-10), and possibly the forced departure from Beroea (Acts 17:13,14).

and please not God,—Although the Jews wanted to please God (Romans 10:2), they were only making themselves obnoxious to Him by opposing His messengers. The use of the present tense verb emphasizes their habitual attitude. Elsewhere Paul says that those who "are in the flesh cannot please God" (Romans 8:8).

and are contrary to all men;—The word "contrary" (Greek: *enantios*) indicates hostility toward another. God had called Israel into existence as a special people that through them He might bless the remainder of mankind. They had proven to be unfaithful which led God to promise a new covenant which would offer blessings to all people. The Jews, however, had allowed the spirit of pride and jealousy to replace the spirit of grace and service. Even the pagans spoke of the Jews cherishing hatred for all others who were not Jewish. It is more likely that here the point is that they are opposed to preaching God's grace to Gentiles as seems clear from the next verse.

V:16 forbidding us to speak to the Gentiles that they may be saved;—"Forbidding" is an explanatory participle more clearly defining what was meant by "contrary to all men." The same attitude on the part of Jews is mentioned in Acts 13:45,50 while Paul was in Antioch of Pisidia and in other places (Acts 14:1-5,19; 17:13; 18:12). Paul himself had displayed the same attitude before his conversion (cf. Acts 26:9-11).

The clause beginning with "that" (Greek: *hina*) shows that the purpose for approaching the Gentiles was that they might be brought to faith and salvation. The verb translated "they may be saved" (Greek: *sozo*) is an aorist passive form which makes it clear that the salvation is a work of God not of man.

42

to fill up their sins always:—The phrase "to fill up" may indicate purpose or result. It seems most likely that both are indicated here. Knowing the course of action among the Jews, God allowed them to continue until the full measure was complete. The natural result of such action as defined in the passage is God's wrath. "Always" is from *pantote* which means "always" or "at all times" or "on every occasion" (Louw & Nida, 67:88). In this place it is a reference to the generations of repeated apostasies and rebellion which reaches the climax with the killing of Jesus Christ and the hindering of the preaching of the message to Gentiles.

but the wrath is come upon them to the uttermost.—The wrath is the wrath of God. Exactly what is meant by the statement is debated. The verb "is come" is the aorist, indicative form of *phthano*. It naturally refers to a past event. In light of other Scripture, it is best to apply the statement to the rejection of Israel as the special people of God. The expression of God's wrath is clearly seen in the work of Jesus who fulfilled the Law and inaugurated the promised Kingdom. That event is closely connected with the beginning of the New Covenant age. The wrath expressed is final so far as the nation is concerned. However, any Jewish person may become a Christian and escape the ultimate wrath of God at the end time through Jesus Christ. The emphatic position of the word "them" in this clause makes it clear that it is the people, the nation, who were recipients of the wrath (cf. Romans 11:11-27). Any effort to apply this statement either to the destruction of Jerusalem in A.D. 70 or to the end of time does violence to the text.

D. CONCERN FOR THE CHURCH, 2:17-3:10

1. Paul's Desire to Return, 2:17-20

V:17 But we, brethren, being bereaved of you for a short season, in presence not in heart, endeavored the more exceedingly to see your face with great desire; V:18 because we would fain have come unto you, I Paul once and again; and Satan hindered us. V:19 For what is our hope, or joy, or crown of glorying? Are not

even ye, before our Lord Jesus at his coming? V:20 For ye are our glory and our joy.

V:17 **But we, brethren, being bereaved of you for a short season,**—The defense started in verse 1 continues. The words here are filled with emotion no doubt because some were saying, or insinuating, that the sudden departure of the preachers was evidence of a lack of real concern for the people whom they had taught. Possibly the thought was expressed that Paul and the others had no intention of returning to visit. The words "but we" mark a contrast between the Jews mentioned above and the writers. The use of "brethren" is a term of affection and is followed by a word expressing the sense of loss at the separation. "Being bereaved" is from a word (Greek: *aporphanizo*) used only here in the New Testament. It means "to make an orphan of someone." Here it is used figuratively of "being separated from" the Christians in Thessalonica. The separation is further emphasized by the following words "of you," or more literally "from (Greek: *apo*) you." Hendriksen translates this phrase as "having been torn away from you" which conveys the thought quite well. "For a short season" may indicate that the writers and the readers had expected the separation to be only for a short time. It did not work out that way and several months may have passed since the preachers had left.

in presence not in heart,—The separation is in body only. This entire section makes it clear that the missionaries loved the converts and the separation had only intensified the awareness of being "bereaved" of them. Their hearts were still very much with those struggling, persecuted, faithful Christians.

endeavored the more exceedingly to see your face with great desire:—The efforts made to return to Thessalonica are not recorded, but from the words used it is evident that there was an eagerness on the part of the missionaries. The word *spudazo* ("endeavored") implies speed, eagerness and seriousness and is intensified by the phrases "more exceedingly" and "with great desire." This is one of the few

44

places where the word "desire" (Greek: *epithumai*) is used in a good sense (cf. also Luke 22:15; Philippians 1:23). Contrary to what seems to have been said about these preachers, the affection for the readers had increased because of the forced separation.

V:18 because we would fain have come unto you, I Paul once and again;—These words give additional affirmation to the truthfulness of verse 17. The verb "would fain" (Greek: *thelo*) expresses a wish. It was evidently chosen to strengthen the emotional element which is so clearly a feature of this passage. The desire to visit Thessalonica had been demonstrated by at least two attempts to do so. The words "I Paul" show the intense personal concern by the apostle. The co-workers had separated at Beroea (Acts 17:14). Timothy had since visited Thessalonica again (1 Thessalonians 3:6), and most likely Silas had either accompanied him or joined him there (Acts 18:5). Paul himself had been unable to return.

and Satan hindered us.—The attempts to revisit Thessalonica had been thwarted by Satan. Satan is the great opposer, or adversary, of God and man; the personal name of the devil. The word "hindered" (Greek: *egkipto*) indicates the use of strong measures in causing someone not to do something. Just how Satan "hindered" Paul is unknown. Many suggestions are found in the commentaries, but the possibilities are too numerous for one to be dogmatic.

V:19 For what is our hope, or joy, or crown of glorying?—The conjunction "for" (Greek: *gar*) introduces the reason for so strongly wanting to be among these people again. It is put in the form of a question, asked not to gain information, but to express the deep feelings more effectively than a mere statement would have done. The friends in Thessalonica filled the writers hearts with hope and joy and glorying—hope that the work begun in them would grow to maturity, joy in the clear genuineness of their faith and glorying as they see the fruit of their labor of preaching the gospel. Paul uses similar terms to refer to converts elsewhere (cf. Romans 1:13; 1 Corinthians 9:2; Philippians 4:1).

The word "crown" (Greek: *stephanos*) refers to the wreath or crown given to the victor in an athletic contest. Victory in such a contest gave grounds for "glorying" or "boasting." This is one of several places that the Christian life is referred to in athletic terms. However, the glorying is not in their work but in God's work through them. These converts from Thessalonica will serve as a "crown," that is, as a basis for glorying at the coming of Jesus Christ.

are not even ye, before our Lord Jesus at his coming?—The words may very well include other Christian groups in addition to the Thessalonians. Here the writers are looking forward to the time when they can stand in the presence of Jesus when He comes at the end time. The word "coming" is from *parousia* which became a technical word for the second coming by the end of the first century. In the New Testament, however, it is used of Paul's personal presence (2 Corinthians 10:10; Philippians 1:26; 2:12), "the coming of Stephanas" (1 Corinthians 16:17), the arrival of Titus (2 Corinthians 7:6,7) as well as the coming of Christ. In the Thessalonian epistles, the word is found in the following verses where it refers to Christ's coming (1 Thessalonians 2:19; 3:13; 4:15; 5:23; 2 Thessalonians 2:1,8). The *parousia* may be described as "personal" since it is the revelation and vindication of Jesus of Nazareth (Acts 1:11). It is inappropriate to think of the *parousia* simply as the physical arrival of a person or as "an historical event in the future" because it not only marks the end of our present historical order but will itself be beyond history, introducing a new order disconnected with the present course of history.

V:20 For ye are our glory and our joy.—This is the final summary statement of their concern for the readers in this section. The words may be translated "Yes truly, you are our glory and our joy." Not only will they be at the end time, they are now, at the time of writing, the glory and joy of the writers.

Chapter 3

2. Timothy sent to help them, 3:1-5

V:1 Wherefore when we could no longer forbear, we thought it good to be left behind at Athens alone; V:2 and sent Timothy, our brother and God's minister in the gospel of Christ, to establish you, and to comfort you concerning your faith; V:3 that no man be moved by these afflictions; for yourselves know that hereunto we are appointed. V:4 For verily, when we were with you, we told you beforehand that we are to suffer affliction: even as it came to pass, and ye know. V:5 For this cause I also, when I could no longer forbear, sent that I might know your faith, lest by any means the tempter had tempted you, and our labor should be in vain.

V:1 Wherefore when we could no longer forbear, we thought it good to be left behind at Athens alone;—"Wherefore" (Greek: *dio*) joins this sentence to what has been said in the preceding paragraph. The purpose is to explain the action now mentioned. Since Paul had been unable to return to Thessalonica, the next best thing was to send Timothy. The feelings and motives of the apostle are made clear in this paragraph. The phrase "when we could no longer forbear" is the translation of a negative circumstantial participle (Greek: *meketi stegontes*) which emphasizes the strong feelings that Paul had for the Thessalonian Christians. The missionaries apparently discussed the matter and decided that Paul would be left alone at Athens while Silas and Timothy made their respective journeys. The use of the plural words is best taken in the normal sense. The co-workers all understood the situation and the loneliness they felt, but were unwilling to gratify personal desires at the expense of the Thessalonians. Silas and Timothy apparently left Athens about the same time.

V:2 and sent Timothy—The one sent is identified and then described. These words refer to the historical event. The use of the plural verb seems to mean that the action was the result of agreement among the missionaries, but the verb in verse 5 below shows that Paul took the immediate action.

our brother and God's minister in the gospel of Christ,— Timothy is called "brother" which underlies the closeness of the relationship among the preachers. This word has no special significance for designating a "church leader" as has been suggested (cf. E. E. Ellis, *Prophecy and Hermeneutic*, 13ff.). Timothy is also "God's minister" (Greek: *diakonos*) which means "one who serves" basically. Some Greek texts have the word *sunergos* ("fellow-worker") instead of *diakonos*, but the overall meaning is not greatly affected either way. Timothy was respected by his co-workers as a diligent, hard-working servant of God, especially in connection with, and in the interest of, the gospel of Christ.

to establish you, and to comfort you concerning your faith;— Here begins the explanation of why Timothy was sent to Thessalonica. First, he was "to establish" (Greek: *sterizo*) them. The verb means "to strengthen, to fix, make firm" or "to confirm one's mind" which was done by providing a support or buttress. Timothy was to "establish" the Thessalonian converts by providing needed mental and spiritual support. The second verb, "to comfort" (Greek: *parakaleo*), means to call to one's side to console and strengthen." Here, in light of verse 3, the thought is more of encouragement and preparation for battle which would involve their faith. The preposition "concerning" (Greek: *huper*) basically means "in behalf of" or "for the sake of" and shows that Timothy's work was to reinforce and strengthen their faith in the midst of affliction. It is clear that a large part of Paul's work was centered in establishing and strengthening the converts wherever he worked (cf. Acts 14:22; 15:32,41; 16:5; 18:23; Romans 1:11; 16:25).

V:3 that no man be moved by these afflictions;—These words introduce a negative purpose which is dependent on the accomplishment of the preceding positive purposes. No one of the Thessalonian Christians would "be moved" if he was effectively established and grounded in the faith. The verb translated "be moved" is from *saino* and is used only here in the New Testament. The word is found with several meanings in secular Greek such as the wagging of a dog's tail, the act of flattery or the shaking of something. Here it is used of the possibility of one being so disturbed that he would give up his beliefs. The cause of such disturbance is what is referred to as "these afflictions." The word *thlipsis* ("affliction") primarily refers to the pressure of hostile opposition and persecution from without. See more on 1:6. The use of the preposition *en*, translated "by" in the ASV, seems to support the idea that the "afflictions" refer more to the methods of opposition being experienced than the opposition itself.

for yourselves know that hereunto we are appointed.—The Thessalonians knew that Christians are going to face opposition without the writers needing to repeat it here. They knew this fact because they had been told by the teachers (see vs. 4). "Know" is from *oidate* which refers to absolute knowledge. The use of *autoi*, translated "yourselves," makes this an emphatic statement. Affliction is not to be thought of as strange and unusual for the Christian, in light of the fact that "we are appointed" to it. The verb translated "are appointed" comes from *keimai* which literally means "I lay." As used here, it has a figurative meaning "I appoint." The word does not indicate an ultimate destiny but a temporary experience appointed as a means to an end. Affliction is the common experience of all who serve God faithfully (2 Timothy 3:12). Knowledge of such suffering keeps the faithful from surprise or dismay (cf. Romans 8:17,18).

V:4 For verily, when we were with you,—The first words of this verse emphasize the truth of the assertion in verse 3. The word "with" (Greek: *pros*) is unusual in a context of this kind, but it emphasizes the "face to face" relationship of the preachers with the hearers.

we told you beforehand that we are to suffer affliction;—While in Thessalonica, the preachers had repeatedly told the converts that they, and all Christians, were to suffer. The imperfect tense of the verb means that the message was repeated over and over. The NASB translates this as "we kept telling you in advance. . ." This seems to have been a common practice from Jesus' time (cf. John 13:19; 14:29; Acts 14:22). The words "we are" come from a verb meaning "I am about to" do something or "to be at the point of doing" something (Greek: *mello*). The significance of the verb here is to show the certainty and divine appointment of tribulation. This expression adds greater certainty to the prediction than a simple future tense. "Affliction" in this verse is from a present passive infinitive which implies both continuing distress and that it will come from an outside agent such as the unbelieving Jews and Gentiles.

even as it came to pass, and ye know.—Here is another appeal to known facts. What had been repeated about the coming affliction came true. That such will come is expected by instructed Christians (1 Peter 4:12-14), who know that affliction produces experience, character and confidence. Passages such as this present an example for preachers and teachers today: basic doctrine should be taught clearly to new converts as they are being prepared for the battles of life in Jesus Christ.

V:5 For this cause I also, when I could no longer forbear, sent that I might know your faith,—"For this cause" gives evidence of the fact that tribulation had already begun among these Christians and that motivated the action by the preachers. The phrase "no longer forbear" is from two words, *meketi* ("no longer") and *stego* ("I put up with" or "I bear up under"). Paul, especially, was concerned about the trouble brought against the new converts, and had been for some time. His patience in the matter came to an end so he sent Timothy in order to learn about the status of their faith. There was no need to repeat the purpose for Timothy's trip already mentioned in verse 2.

lest by any means the tempter had tempted you,— Paul's haunting fear is now revealed. The words "the tempter" are from a participle which literally means "the one tempting" or "this one who tempts," and it certainly refers to Satan. Matthew alone uses this same designation for Satan elsewhere in the New Testament (Matthew 4:3). Earlier in this epistle Satan is spoken of as hindering the missionaries' plans to return to Thessalonica. Paul often spoke of Satan and each time it is clear that someone real is meant. Here also "the tempter," Satan, is presented as a great and dangerous spiritual enemy. It is clear that Satan does tempt people and constantly attempts to frustrate the work of God. "Had tempted" is from an aorist indicative verb (Greek: *peirazo*) which here means that Satan had, before the writing of this epistle, already tempted the Thessalonian Christians. The question that concerned Paul at the time was whether the tempting had been successful in leading them into sin.

and our labor should be in vain.— Paul's uncertainty just mentioned is pointed out again. The use of the aorist subjunctive verb (the mood of moderate contingency) shows that the return of Timothy from Thessalonica brought the good news that the underlying confidence of the missionaries was justified.

All questions about an inconsistency of attitude about the true conversion of the Thessalonians are unfounded. The assurance of conversion is clear in 1:2-6 and the concern in 3:5 is perfectly consistent with other New Testament teaching. Contrary to Hendriksen and others, it is possible for "God's truly chosen ones" to sin and be eternally lost (cf. 1 Corinthians 10:12; Hebrews 2:1,2; 6:4-6; 10:26-31). The fear of that possibility had weighed heavily on Paul's mind until he was unwilling to wait longer to send Timothy for information about them.

3. Timothy's report, 3:6-10

V:6 But when Timothy came even now unto us from you, and brought us glad tidings of your faith and love, and that ye have good remembrance of us always, longing to see us, even as we also to see you; **V:7** for this cause, brethren, we were comforted over you in all our distress and affliction through your faith: **V:8** for now we live, if ye stand fast in the Lord. **V:9** For what thanksgiving can we render again unto God for you, for all the joy wherewith we joy for your sakes before our God; **V:10** night and day praying exceedingly that we may see your face, and may perfect that which is lacking in your faith?

This section of the epistle breathes an attitude of happiness. After clearly describing the desire for information about the Thessalonians, the writers describe their state of mind now that Timothy has returned to them.

V:6 But when Timothy came even now unto us from you,— Evidently this epistle was written as soon as possible after Timothy reported what he had learned. The words "even now" are from *arti*, an adverb of coincidence which indicates strictly present time, as contrasted with past or future time. It may be translated as "just, just now, this moment, even now." The use of this word shows the intense concern of the writers. The expression that Timothy came "unto us from you" is more personal than saying "Timothy returned." This letter is very personal and shows the deep love and care of the writers in many ways.

and brought us glad tidings of your faith and love,— Here is an instance of a non-technical use of the verb *euaggelizomai* ("brought glad tidings"). This word is normally used in the New Testament of the preaching of the gospel. Timothy's news was so very important at the time that the authors chose the greatest word at their command to express joy. The good news was concerning the "faith and love" demonstrated in the lives of the Christians in Thessalonica. The faith and love mentioned in 1:3 is still present among them. See Galatians 5:6 for the same thought. The absence of the word "hope" is no doubt significant in view of the content of the section beginning at 4:13.

and that ye have good remembrance of us always, longing to see us,—The second part of the report by Timothy relates to the personal attitude of the Thessalonian Christians toward the preachers. The adjective "good" (Greek: *agathos*) does not merely indicate that the Thessalonians had not forgotten the missionaries, but that the memory was happy and friendly. The alternative would be to remember them with bitterness because of the trouble they had brought. The good memory is emphasized by the use of the word "always." The Christians of Thessalonica were also "longing to see" the missionaries. The word "longing" is from *epipotheo*, a strong word and has within it the thought of "yearning after." It is a present tense verb and shows that the "longing" was constant. This word was a favorite with Paul, it seems, since he uses it seven of the nine times it is found in the New Testament.

even as we also to see you;—The desire to be reunited was mutual. "Even as" (Greek: *kathaper*) makes clear that the longing is equal on both sides. The preservation of the affectionate relationship was important for Paul and his co-workers.

V:7 for this cause, brethren, we were comforted over you in all our distress and affliction through your faith:—"For this cause" calls attention to what has just been said. The use of the singular sums up the faith, the love and the good memories along with the desire to see them. The use of "brethren: once again brings out the strong affection for the readers. "We were comforted" is from a word (Greek: *parakaleo*) which means "to call to one's side" for the purpose of "exhorting, comforting, and encouraging." The use of the aorist tense shows that comfort became a reality in the writers by the report given by Timothy. "Over you" shows that the comfort experienced was based directly on the Thessalonians. They were the ground for the comfort received by the missionaries "in all our distress and affliction." These two nouns are linked together by the use of only one definite article, and because of that they form two aspects of the entire difficult situation. "Distress" (Greek: *anagke*) basically means "necessity" or "constraint" and here refers to some compulsion that forces itself upon one. It may be financial needs or some unknown external constraint, or possibly the pressure of the work of tent-making. "Affliction" (Greek: *thlipsis*) refers to crushing troubles which are heaped upon one by others such as persecutions. The same word is in 1:6 and 3:3. See the comments on those verses.

The prepositional phrase "through your faith" states the means by which the comfort was brought to the missionaries. *Dia* ("through" or "by means of") is evidently used to express intermediate agency here and the word points to the means by which the comfort came. The actual means was "your faith." The point is that Paul and his co-workers were comforted by the news that the faith of the new converts had held firm in the face of problems. This is the fourth time in this chapter that the faith of these people has been mentioned. "Faith" speaks of personal and absolute reliance upon the Lord Jesus Christ for salvation. Faith is not all there is to Christianity, but it is basic.

V:8 for now we live,— Paul, and to some extent his co-workers, had been under a heavy burden of apprehension which drained him. But "now" (Greek: *nun*), in consequence of the report by Timothy, "we live" (Greek: *zomen*). "We live" seems to indicate more the thought "we now enjoy life" than simple living. The contrast with the former state is vivid. The use of the present tense verb indicates that this is not merely a momentary reaction but a continuing fact. The life is not some mysterious communication of life as Best suggests (pp. 142-3). A modern writer might say something like: "It was a shot in the arm."

if ye stand fast in the Lord.—The use of *ean* instead of *ie* for "if" is a little unusual but seems merely to emphasize the facts of Timothy's report and implicitly admonishes the Thessalonians to continue in the faith. The words "stand fast" are from *steko*, a word that means "to stand firm" with an emphasis on firmness. The word "ye" is an emphatic word for the Thessalonians in this context. "In the Lord" points to the sphere of the desired steadfastness. On the basis of faith they had entered into the Christian family and they needed to hold to that faith in all respects.

V:9 For what thanksgiving can we render again unto God for you,—The conjunction "for" (Greek: *gar*) explains the acceptance of the news of the steadfastness of the young Christians in Thessalonica as life in verse 8. The question which begins here continues through verse 10 and is rhetorical and implies that Paul and his friends feel utterly unable to give back to God anything equal to their joy. The word translated "render again" (Greek: *antapodidomi*) is a compound word used in reference to thanksgiving to God only here in the New Testament. The full meaning of the word is "to give back something in return for something received. The thanksgiving is "to God" and is "for" or "concerning you," i.e. all the Christians in Thessalonica. The attitude of thanksgiving is mentioned repeatedly in these epistles (cf. 1 Thessalonians 1:2; 2:13; 2 Thessalonians 1:3; 2:13).

for all the joy wherewith we joy for your sakes before our God;— By using *epi* ("for") to introduce this statement the ground or reason for the thanksgiving is made clear. The "distress and affliction" on the part of the writers (vs. 7) has been fully recompensed and brings a new awareness of joy because of the faithfulness of the Thessalonians. This joy is a continuing fact as indicated by the use of the present tense verb (Greek: *chairo*). The joy being experienced by the writers is "before our God." This is a joy coming from the sense of God's presence and is free from any personal selfishness or worldly motives. The phrase "before our God" or "in the presence of our God" expressed with the word *emprosthen* is more common in 1 Thessalonians than any other of Paul's epistles.

V:10 night and day praying exceedingly—The praying of the writers is described by two adjuncts standing emphatically before the participle, praying, in the Greek text. The praying is said to be offered "night and day." Both the nouns are in the genitive case which shows that the praying was done during the night and during the day, not all night and all day. For the same structure, see 2:9 above. The word "exceedingly" (Greek: *huperekperissou*) is found only two other times in the

New Testament (1 Thessalonians 5:13; Ephesians 3:20). It means "abundantly, beyond all measure, exceedingly overflowing all bounds, super abundantly." The praying of the writers of this epistle was not halfhearted, but was exuberant and intensely earnest. The twofold description of their praying is in perfect harmony with the word translated praying. That verb means "to ask, to beg" and it indicates a feeling of need on the part of the ones asking. The grammatical structure shows that the asking is subsidiary to the desire to adequately thank God.

that we may see your face, and may perfect that which is lacking in your faith?—The writers wanted to see the readers in person. They wanted to see the readers but not for personal gratification, but for the benefit of the readers. The word "perfect" (Greek: *katartizo*) is used elsewhere of mending nets (Matthew 4:21; Mark 1:19) and is translated "restore" in Galatians 6:1. It sometimes means "to furnish completely, equip, prepare." The words "that which is lacking in your faith" do not necessarily mean something was wrong with their faith (cf. verses 6-8), rather here the implication is that there were important areas in which they needed further instruction. Some of these areas are indicated in 4:13-5:22. Since there was little chance that they would actually see the Thessalonians, these matters are covered in this epistle. This lack evidently was caused by the abrupt end of the preaching and teaching when the missionaries were forced to leave (Acts 17:10).

E. Paul's prayer, 3:11-13

V:11 Now may our God and Father himself, and our Lord Jesus, direct our way unto you: V:12 and the Lord make you to increase and abound in love one toward another, and toward all men, even as we also do toward you; V:13 to the end he may establish your hearts unblamable in holiness before our God and Father, at the coming of our Lord Jesus with all his saints.

V:11 Now may our God and Father himself, and our Lord Jesus,—The desire to return to Thessalonica is repeated. Satan had hindered such a visit, but God is mightier than Satan and may see fit to allow the missionaries to return. The words emphasize that it is God who must open the way, not themselves. The close association of God the Father and Jesus here is significant. They share the prerogative of deity to direct the way of the people (cf. Psalm 32:8; 37:23). By joining the Father and Son in prayer illustrates the fact that Christians generally accepted the Son as deity.

direct our way unto you:—The verb "direct" (Greek: *kateuthuno*) is used so that it expresses a wish or strong desire. Its basic meaning is "I make straight" or "I put in the right way, I direct." It is used in two other New Testament passages, Luke 1:79 and 2 Thessalonians 3:5. Moffatt says that the verb is common in this sense of providence directing human actions (*Expositors Greek Testament*). If the prayer was answered, the preachers would have been able to return to Thessalonica without detours or deviations from their path. The missionaries were certainly aware of the fact that it is God's prerogative to determine the time and manner in which the prayer might be answered.

V:12 and the Lord make you to increase and abound in love— The conjunction at the beginning of this verse is adversative and probably should be translated "but." The sense is "whatever may be the situation for the writers, as for you, may the Lord. . ." The writers recognized that the spiritual growth of the readers was not in their hands but God's. "The Lord" might refer either to God the Father or to the Son in verse 11. From the context and Paul's normal use of the word, it is most likely that Lord refers to Jesus in this place (cf. vss. 8 and 11). The authors use two more optative verbs in expressing their prayer for the readers. The verbs "increase" and "abound" are practically synonymous and the combination strengthens the idea so that the meaning may be stated as "increase to overflowing." "In love" refers to the love already in these Christians (1:3; 3:6), and the prayer is that it may grow to greater proportions. The characteristics of this love are found in 1 Corinthians 13 and it is to be developed in every Christian's life.

one toward another, and toward all men,—The same phrase is found in 5:15 in a slightly different context. There seems to be no ground for the suggestion that there were two distinct groups in the Thessalonian church—a Jewish group and a Gentile group (K. Lake, *The Earlier Epistles of St. Paul,* pp. 89-90). The words "one toward another" are best taken as referring to the fellow Christians (cf. John 13:34; 1 Peter 1:22; 1 John 3:14; 4:7,8,20,21) and "toward all men" to the wider circle of the human race (cf. Galatians 6:10; 2 Peter 1:7). The Christian obligation to love and serve must not be limited to fellow Christians but to all even if they persecute you (Matthew 5:44).

even as we also do toward you;—The missionaries followed Christ's instructions, but appeal to their own example as one to be followed by the converts. Here is one more comment that emphasizes the love of Paul and his co-workers for the readers.

This chapter closes, as does every other chapter of this epistle, with a direct reference to the coming of the Lord at the end of this world system.

V:13 to the end he may establish your hearts—"To the end" is *eis* with the articular infinitive of purpose, *to sterixai.* The word "establish" (Greek: *sterizo*) means "to make stable" or "to place firmly" (see 3:2). The word "heart" does not refer only to the emotional side of man's nature, as in our use of the term, but the place where the hidden motives of life and conduct take shape. The word "he" is not in the Greek text but is added for clarity. The "Lord" is the one who establishes men and it is only as He develops in them the necessary inner spiritual stability that they will be able to stand firm and unmoved regardless of what the future holds.

unblamable in holiness—"Unblamable" (Greek: *amemptos*) means "blameless, without blame, innocent, guiltless." "In holiness" (Greek: *en hagiosune*) refers to "the sphere in which blamelessness is to be shewn" (Alford, III:267). The "holiness" spoken of is the state of sanctity rather than the process of becoming holy (*hagiosune,* not *hagiasmos*). This state is brought about initially by one's entering a right relationship with God through Jesus Christ. Christians are responsible to maintain that relationship and to nurture it by developing the life style which demonstrates the fact of a life set apart to God's service.

before our God and Father,—To be blameless in God's sight is much more important than being blameless before men. Men judge as critics, but God as a loving Father. The words of the text have an eschatological character as is clear from the next phrase.

at the coming of our Lord Jesus with all his saints.— Blamelessness is the goal for Christians in this life, but it will have its full realization at the Lord's return. It is only those who have accepted the historical Jesus of the New Testament as God's Son and their Savior, who will be found acceptable ("blameless") at the end.

The word "coming" is from *parousia* a word denoting "a personal presence alongside of" someone or thing. This is one of the most common words in the New Testament used to refer to the coming of Jesus Christ at the end of this world system. It refers to His abiding presence which will be a time of blessing for His people (see on 2:19). *Parousia* may well be the key word of this epistle, a word of hope, cheer, comfort and blessing, speaking great assurance to the people of God who were undergoing severe trials.

with all his saints.—These words have been the center of much discussion. The word "saints" could be translated as "holy ones" as in the New International Version. This opens the debate as to whether the angels, the saints, or both are intended. Good arguments have been made for each view.

The Greek Old Testament (the Septuagint) has the same words *hoi hagioi* when angels are referred to (cf. Deuteronomy 33:3; Zechariah 14:5). In the New Testament, Jesus is represented as coming "with the holy angels" (Mark 8:38; 13:27; Matthew 25:31). Angels are also spoken of in connection with the revelation of Jesus Christ (2 Thessalonians 1:7). Because of these and other similar passages, several recognized scholars conclude that in this verse angels are intended (See Marshall, pp. 102-103 for an example).

Those who think "saints" is the best translation think that the reference is to human spirits, the "holy dead" whose spirits the Lord will bring with Himself at His return. The argument is based on the fact that *hagioi* is the standard New Testament word for those who have been cleansed by the blood of Jesus Christ. Only in Jude 14 does "holy ones" refer to angels in the New Testament unless it does in this verse. Paul consistently uses this expression for saints, although it is referring to saints on earth. Those who hold the view that saints is the proper reading ask why an exception to the normal use be made here so that "angels" is read (See Hendriksen, pp. 92-94 for an example).

Several well-respected writers think that both angels and redeemed believers are included in this statement. Leon Morris is representative of this group. He says,

> In this particular case there seems no reason for holding that Paul's thought is limited to the one class or the other. It is clear from the New Testament that both angels and the departed saints will be associated with the Lord when He returns" (p. 115).

Since there is no specific mention of angels in 1 Thessalonians and since there is no connection of angels with anything in this epistle, but there are references to glorified believers, it is my conclusion that the reference is to redeemed men instead of angels. This position does not exclude the attendance of angels at the Lord's return as Mark 8:38 says. Of course, the attempts to connect this statement with the so-called rapture are to be dismissed.

Chapter 4

IV. INSTRUCTIONS ABOUT HOW TO LIVE, 4:1-5:11

A. The Problem of Sexual Immorality, 4:1-8

V:1 Finally then, brethren, we beseech and exhort you in the Lord Jesus, that, as ye received of us how ye ought to walk and to please God, even as ye do walk,—that ye abound more and more. V:2 For ye know what charge we gave you through the Lord Jesus. V:3 For this is the will of God, even your sanctification, that ye abstain from fornication; V:4 that each one of you know how to possess himself of his own vessel in sanctification and honor, V:5 not in the passion of lust, even as the Gentiles who know not God; V:6 that no man transgress, and wrong his brother in the matter: because the Lord is an avenger in all these things, as also we forewarned you and testified. V:7 For God called us not for uncleanness, but in sanctification. V:8 Therefore he that rejecteth, rejecteth not man, but God, who giveth his Holy Spirit unto you.

V:1 Finally then, brethren,—"Finally" does not necessarily imply that the end of the epistle is near. It does mark the transition in subject matter. Having been hindered from speaking to the readers in person, the recent converts are addressed in writing so that what was lacking may be supplied (see note on 3:10). "Then" is from *oun*, a word which expresses consequence or simple sequence. As the writers had prayed that the readers might grow in holiness, they now exhort them to the same end. The use of "brethren" shows their tenderness in approaching some very delicate subjects.

we beseech and exhort you in the Lord Jesus,—"We beseech" is from a word that basically means "to ask" or "request." This is another indication of personal interest by the writers. It is interesting that in Paul's writings this word is used only in epistles to the Macedonian churches (5:12; 2 Thessalonians 2:1; Philippians 4:3). "You" is a plural form and includes all the Christians in Thessalonica. "Exhort" is from a compound Greek word which, in this context, means "to exhort in the sense of urging or encouraging" (Lineberry, 38). "Beseech" and "exhort" are used together only here in the New Testament and express the urgency of maintaining the Christian life style.

in the Lord Jesus,—These words seem to carry the idea that the writers have authority, but more that since the readers are "in the Lord," that itself should be motive enough to follow the teaching from them. The readers should have a sense that Jesus Christ is very much involved in the situation.

that,—This conjunction (Greek: *hina*) is left hanging for the present, but is repeated and the thought completed at the end of the sentence.

as ye received of us how ye ought to walk—"Received" indicates that the missionaries had taught clearly, not only the basic message of salvation (2:13), but also the matters of ethical conduct. The word "ought" is from *dei* which indicates a moral obligation based on what they had received. "To walk" is a common New Testament phrase for one's way of life. The use of the present tense emphasizes that proper conduct is to be a continuous fact of life.

and to please God,—This connects very closely with the words "to walk." The two infinitives "to walk and to please God" form a hendiadys (the co-ordination of two ideas, one of which is dependent on the other) and mean "to walk so as to please God." Being what God wants us to be is a full-time spiritual exercise.

even as ye do walk,—The flow of thought is interrupted again evidently because the writers wanted to make sure that the readers did not think they were being condemned. The writers word this phrase so that praise and encouragement are clearly given because the readers had been living in harmony with the instructions given as Timothy's report showed.

that ye abound more and more.—The *hina* is repeated and its clause completed. The verb "abound" (Greek: *perisseuo*) is used in 3:12 where it is used of abounding "in love." Generally this verb is used with some specific quality which is to abound. Here the instructions are dealing with the whole of life and the point is that the Christians were to grow continually in Christ-likeness. Some specific areas will be mentioned later.

V:2 For ye know—This phrase is used over and over in this epistle (cf. 1:5; 2:1,2,5,11; 3:3,4) to emphasize that no new message is given, but the statements are to refresh the memory of the readers. Repetition is one of the major factors in learning.

what charge we gave you through the Lord Jesus,—"Charge" is actually a plural word in the Greek text. The word has a military background and is generally used in the New Testament to show an authoritative note. The apostolic teaching is not to be treated with indifference because it was delivered by the authority of the Lord Jesus Christ. This is clearly indicated by the last phrase "through the Lord Jesus." The apostolic teaching did not originate in the apostles, it came from the Lord and is to be obeyed.

V:3 For this is the will of God,—"For" (Greek: *gar*) is explanatory and shows that the charges given to the converts did not originate with the writers of the epistle. "This" is the subject and is emphatically placed in the sentence. The word refers to what follows and is a further explanation of the "charges" mentioned above in verse 2. "Will" translates *thelema* and is used here without the article evidently indicating that what follows is not the entire will of God on everything.

even your sanctification,—"Sanctification" (Greek: *hagiasmos*) is in apposition with "will." God's will for the Thessalonians in this context is their sanctification. This is the earliest known occurrence of this word in Christian literature. It is used of consecration to some religious purpose in earlier Greek writing, but even in the Greek translation of the Old Testament it does not bear the strong ethical sense it has here. Christians are to be wholly set apart for God and separated by life and conduct from the unbelieving world.

that ye abstain from fornication;—"Abstain" is from a word that means "to hold back, keep off, to abstain." Note the use of this word in Acts 15:20 where Silas was involved in carrying a letter to the churches. That these Christians in Thessalonica were told to "abstain from fornication" may seem strange to modern readers, but such a warning was very much needed among first century converts from paganism. Among many pagans various forms of extramarital sexual union were encouraged. Certain forms of religious rituals involved *porneia*. This word primarily means "to engage in sexual immorality of any kind, often with the implication of prostitution," but is used in the New Testament to refer to any form of illicit sexual relationship. Here it is the broad meaning which is to be accepted. From the beginning Christianity has sanctified sexual union within marriage as did Judaism; outside marriage it was, and is, forbidden. Such restrictions would be difficult for a pagan man to accept. It would not be surprising that some slipped back into old habits after conversion. Compare similar teaching in 1 Corinthians 1:4-9; 5:1-5; 6:12-20 given to people from basically a pagan background.

V:4 that each one of you know how—Having stated the negative side of God's will for them, the writers turn to the positive. Each individual should "know," or "learn so that he knows."

to possess himself of his own vessel—Several problems are raised by these words. Do the words mean "to gain mastery over his body" (NEB; cf. NIV), or "to take a wife for himself" (RSV)? The latter view was held by some early writers, like

Theodore of Mopsuestia who died in 428 and Augustine who died in 430. The word translated "to possess" (Greek: *ktaomai*) is a present tense infinitive. When used in combination with "vessel" (Greek: *skeuos*), it is an idiom, a euphemistic manner of referring to sexual relations. The word "vessel" in this verse may refer to one's wife or to one's body theoretically, but it is the latter possibility that fits the context best. There is no New Testament example of a man's wife being called his *skeuos*. Such a description would be degrading to her.

The proper view of this statement is that each man must "know how to possess," that is "to control," his own body. This is in harmony with other uses of the word "vessel" in Paul's writings as well as other Biblical uses. Nowhere in the New Testament is the wife or husband said to be the "vessel" of the other.

in sanctification and honor,— Man's body belongs to the Lord and should be consecrated to Him (cf. 1 Corinthians 6:20). Sanctification excludes impurity, and impurity dishonors the body so the admonition is to control one's body lest he be dishonored (cf. Romans 1:24).

V:5 not in the passion of lust,—The body belongs to the Lord and is not to be used as an instrument of self-indulgence. The word "passion" (Greek: *pathos*) is never neutral in the New Testament, but always has a bad sense. It means "an affection of the mind, emotion or passion." "Lust" (Greek: *epithumai*) means "desire, craving, longing." It is used mostly in a bad sense as here. "Passion" presents the passive side of a vice, an ungovernable desire, and "lust" the active side of the vice. The two together indicate the surrender of a person to his passions.

even as the Gentiles who know not God;—The Gentiles (i.e., pagans), those who know nothing of the law of Moses or Christian behavior, know nothing of the holy and honorable conduct urged on these readers. Paul uses the expression "who know not God" often to refer to non-Jewish people. In Romans 1:18ff., there is a fuller description of the Gentile's status. They had at one time knowledge of God, but had at some point "refused to have God in their knowledge" (Romans 1:28). The result was, and is, that without some positive knowledge of God, one will not live a sanctified Christian life.

V:6 that no man transgress, and wrong his brother in the matter:—Those who take this as continuing the discussion of sexual purity have the much stronger basis. The word "transgress" (used only here in the New Testament) is an infinitive form which literally means "to go beyond" and here means the crossing of a forbidden boundary, and therefore, trespassing (sexually) on territory which is not one's own. The transgression spoken of is one that wrongs a brother. "Wrong" (Greek: *pleonekteo*) means "take advantage of, overreach, defraud." The word speaks of the desire to possess more than one should have in any area of life. The meaning here is that one should not take his brother's wife, or other member of his household, and use her to satisfy his lust. The words "in the matter" certainly refer to the matter under discussion, not to some new topic. The words "his brother" seem to refer to a fellow Christian, although the same truth applies if they refer to a physical brother or to a pagan.

because the Lord is an avenger in all these things, as also we forewarned you and testified.—"Because" introduces at least one reason for the admonitions given. "Avenger" (Greek: *ekdikos*) refers to one who metes out justice. Here it refers to the Lord Jesus Christ, it seems, since the subject is changed to God in verse seven. Paul's usage of the word in a judgment context is generally referring to Jesus Christ (cf. 2 Thessalonians 1:8; 1 Corinthians 4:5). Once again the readers are reminded that such matters had already been taught them while the missionaries were in Thessalonica (see above 2:11,12). The final word in this verse is a strong one and may be translated "we insisted" or "we solemnly testified."

V:7 For God called us not for uncleanness,—A second reason for the admonitions is given now. God had called the converts to something better than "uncleanness" (Greek: *akatharsia*), a word which implies "impurity" in either the physical or moral sense. Here it is the latter which also confirms that sexual purity is still the subject. The word "called" points to a specific event which was when the readers heard the word and obeyed the gospel (cf. 2 Thessalonians 2:14).

but in sanctification.—"Sanctification" is the same word as in verse 4 and is something that happens at conversion and is developed as one grows into Christlikeness. The Christian is to live his life in conscious devotion to God. Note that it is God who calls, and He has a claim on His people.

V:8 Therefore—This is a compound particle and is very emphatic. It directs attention to the conclusion which follows more forcibly than more common words could. This word is found only here and in Hebrews 12:1 in the New Testament.

he that rejecteth,—These words address any one who might reject or set aside the charge (vs. 2) or the standards in verses 4 and 5 and, as a result, does not obey them.

rejecteth not man, but God,—"Man" is a general reference and means any man who rejects the message. When Jesus Christ charged His apostles and sent them out to preach, He made it clear that they represented Him so that when someone refused to hear their message he refused to hear Christ as well as the Father (Luke 10:16; Matthew 10:40). Behind the instructions given by Paul and his co-workers was God, and to disregard the instructions is a rejection of Him.

who giveth his Holy Spirit unto you.—God gives His Holy Spirit to all who obey Him (Acts 5:32). The present tense verb is used to indicate the character of God; He is the giver. The position of the adjective "Holy" puts an emphasis on the word. Since the Spirit given to each Christian is Holy, the demand for practical holiness in the lives of those in whom He dwells is understood (cf. 1 Corinthians 6:19,20).

B. The problem of social conduct, 4:9-12

V:9 But concerning love of the brethren ye have no need that one write unto you: for ye yourselves are taught of God to love one another; V:10 for indeed ye do it toward all the brethren that are in all Macedonia. But we exhort you, brethren, that ye abound more and more; V:11 and that ye study to be quiet, and to do your own business, and to work with your hands, even as

we charged you; V:12 that ye may walk becomingly toward them that are without, and may have need of nothing.

V:9 But concerning love of the brethren—The words "but concerning" are normally used in Paul to introduce an answer to a question asked in a letter (cf. 1 Corinthians 7:1,25; 8:1; 12:1; 16:1,12). Several writers have suggested that the Thessalonian church had sent a letter by Timothy or, possibly, independently (G. Milligan, 126; Frame, 141 for examples). This suggestion is a possibility, but there is no evidence for such a letter unless it is this phrase. If Timothy had brought the question as a part of his report, the response would have been given in the same way. The context does not indicate a question from the readers, but it does indicate that some of the Christians were not living up to the proper standards of Christian conduct. These words seem to be more of a spontaneous admonition on the point.

The words "love of the brethren" (Greek: *philadelphia*) are usually restricted to love for fellow-Christians in the New Testament, whereas "love" (Greek: *agape*) is to be extended to all people (cf. 3:12).

ye have no need that one write unto you:—These words suggest a contrast with the matters of the preceding section, concerning which there apparently was such a need.

for ye yourselves are taught of God to love one another;— "For" is used to introduce an explanation and the words "ye yourselves" put an emphasis on the readers. They "are taught of God." The word translated "taught of God" (Greek: *theodidaktos*) is found only here in the New Testament and this is apparently the first time it was used in Greek literature. It does not mean that they were taught directly by God apart from the preachers, Paul, Silvanus and Timothy. These men were guided by the Holy Spirit to speak God's words. To accept that teaching was to accept God. The people were taught "to love one another," and, in fact, the writers of this epistle had already spoken of their love (3:6) and had prayed that it might "increase and abound" (3:12). The words in this verse indicate a love that is self-sacrificing because of the object of the love, "one another."

V:10 for indeed you do it toward all the brethren that are in all Macedonia.—Again the writers recognize that the Thessalonian Christians did in fact love "one another" in all the area of Macedonia. Evidently they had used the lines of communication between their city and other places in the province (cf. 1:7,8).

But we exhort you, brethren, that ye abound more and more;—After implicitly praising the readers, Paul and his co-workers "exhort" them to abound even more. "Exhort" is from *parakaleo*. This word is discussed at 4:1 along with the phrase "abound more and more." The faithful Christians may not rest in any measure of attainment, but are to always be stretching out for more Christlikeness in loving one another.

V:11 and that ye study to be quiet,—The exhortation to abound in love toward the brethren is followed by a series of infinitive phrases exhorting the readers regarding other matters which may be considered as the fruit of love for the brethren. First, the word "study" is from a present infinitive indicating a continuing attitude and action. The word basically means "to earnestly aspire to something, implying strong ambition for some goal" (Louw and Nida). The second present infinitive is translated "to be quiet," a word which basically means "to be at rest" or "silent." Here it indicates a calm spirit or inner tranquility. Bruce points out that it is something of an oxymoron to connect these two words. However, it seems that the excessive interest in the end time had brought about a restless excitement among the Thessalonian Christians which made them disinterested in doing the ordinary things of daily living. Many had become idle, it seems.

and to do your own business,—Another present tense infinitive emphasizing continuous action is used. This admonition is more specific than to be quiet. Each was to mind his or her own personal affairs. This is a warning against meddling in the affairs of others. Certainly they are to be concerned about the needs of others, but they must avoid the neglect of their own responsibilities. Note 2 Thessalonians 3:11; 1 Timothy 5:13; 1 Peter 4:14 for similar teaching.

and to work with your hands,—This present infinitive, "to work," means "to labor" and, beyond doubt, manual labor is meant. It refers to the basic responsibility of the daily work required to earn a living. The writers knew that pious idlers can be a serious danger to the peace of a congregation or the brotherhood. Remember the example of hard work done by Paul and his co-workers to support themselves while in Thessalonica (2:9).

even as we charged you;—The Thessalonians had been "charged" to be honorably independent. "Charged" (Greek: *paraggello*) is an aorist tense which refers to definite action in the past. Paul and the others had given the charge, command, or order, while they were in Thessalonica. The use of "even as" here insists upon the exact correspondence between those commands and the present ones.

V:12 that ye may walk becomingly toward them that are without,—The first purpose for the charge above was that the Christians conduct themselves ("walk") "becomingly," a word that means in an honorable manner so as to cause no offense to the unbelievers. This concern with example is found repeatedly in the New Testament (cf. 2:12; 4:1; Romans 13:13; 1 Corinthians 5:12,13; 10:32,33; 14:40; Colossians 4:5; 1 Timothy 3:7; 1 Peter 2:12). It is impossible for the faithful Christian to live without regard to appearances.

and may have need of nothing.—The word translated "nothing" (Greek: *medeis*) may be either masculine, "no one," or neuter, "nothing." If it is taken as masculine as the RSV and NIV do, the point is that as the Christians follow the charges given in the context they will lead respectable lives and be independent citizens rather than parasites. It is argued that the masculine word would focus more on the abuse of brotherly love (Mare, 275) and fits the context better (Marshall 117). On the other hand, the expression "have need of" is generally used with the genitive of the "thing" needed, that is, the "thing" needed is in the genitive case, it seems that it should be taken as a neuter here. The neuter stresses that the readers are to make proper provision for themselves and their families by their personal labor. There may be times of need in any family, but it should not be of their own choosing. Those who deliberately impose upon the generosity of others are not living in love.

C. The problem about those who had died, 4:13-18

V:13 But we would not have you ignorant, brethren, concerning them that fall asleep; that ye sorrow not, even as the rest, who have no hope. V:14 For if we believe that Jesus died and rose again, even so them also that are fallen asleep in Jesus will God bring with him. V:15 For this we say unto you by the word of the Lord, that we that are alive, that are left unto the coming of the Lord, shall in no wise precede them that are fallen asleep. V:16 For the Lord himself shall descend from heaven, with a shout, with the voice of the archangel, and with the trump of God: and the dead in Christ shall rise first; V:17 then we that are alive, that are left, shall together with them be caught up in the clouds, to meet the Lord in the air: and so shall we ever be with the Lord. V:18 Wherefore comfort one another with these words.

V:13 But we would not have you ignorant, brethren,—The use of "but" (Greek: *de*) and "brethren" with the words "we would not have you ignorant" all point to the beginning of a new topic. These latter words are common in Paul's writings. He uses them to introduce an explanation for a statement (Romans 11:25), to justify a warning (1 Corinthians 10:1), to introduce personal matters (Romans 1:13; 2 Corinthians 1:8). Here he uses the phrase to introduce a new topic and to give fresh information about something the readers had already been told. The phrase is equal to another used by Paul, "I would have you to know" (Colossians 2:11; cf. Philippians 1:12).

concerning them that fall asleep;—The content of this paragraph indicates that since Paul and his fellow preachers had left Thessalonica, at least one of the new converts had died. That raised the question about the state of the dead in relation to those still alive: Do they miss out on some blessing?

The words "them that fall asleep" are from a participle in the present tense and refers to "them that fall asleep from time to time." The word "asleep" is used to refer to death for believers several times in the New Testament (Matthew 27:52; John 11:11-13; Acts 7:60; 1 Corinthians 7:39; 15:6,18) and the thought seems to be in the words "rest from their labors" in Revelation 14:13. The comparison is appropriate in implying rest from labor and also the awakening in the resurrection. Of course, the sleep in this context has nothing to do with the doctrine that the soul is in unconscious repose (soul-sleep). The state of the soul after death is not in the context, but the body is thought of as being asleep and no longer in communication with its earthly environment.

that ye sorrow not, even as the rest, who have no hope.—These words do not indicate that the living believed the dead mentioned are lost. The problem is in the failure to understand the true status of the dead believers. The readers would be expected to grieve over the death of a loved one, but the words here mean that "they are not to continue grieving." The Christian who understands the true condition may well grieve because of personal loss but at the same time rejoice because the departed has gone to be with the Lord (cf. Philippians 1:23). The grieving which is spoken about here is like that of the pagan who is without hope. The pagan thought that when one died that was it. Such a view is well attested in contemporary literature. According to one Theocritus "hopes are for the living; the dead are without hope." There were a few statements about immortality in pagan literature but there was no real glory attached to the thought. Paul mentions the same thought in Ephesians 2:12. The Christian's hope is of a resurrection because Jesus was raised.

Some of the Christians in Thessalonica had evidently misunderstood some things they had been taught. They seem to have missed the fact that God's blessings are not reserved for the ones who will still be living on earth at Christ's coming. Those blessings are also for the believers who have died.

V:14 For if we believe that Jesus died and rose again,—The writers are so certain of the fact of Jesus' resurrection that they put this statement in the form of a conditional sentence.

72

No doubt is indicated by the word "if." The sense is "if we believe that Jesus died and rose again, and He did." The use of "Jesus" in this sentence is important because it reminds the readers that Jesus, a man, died (an actual historical event). If that man died and rose again, why sorrow like pagans who do not accept that fact? Christ's resurrection is the guarantee of the Christian's hope.

even so them also that are fallen asleep in Jesus will God bring with him.—"Even so" (Greek: *houtos*) is an adverb and indicates that those who believe that Jesus rose should in the same manner believe that they will be raised at the end time. "In Jesus" is literally "through Jesus" (Greek: *dia tou iesou*). Since the preposition *dia* is nowhere else translated "in," it seems best to translate it "through" in this place also. Either translation leaves some questions about the specific meaning of the statement. The phrase "through Jesus" may connect with the verb "will bring" and would give the sense as "even so, through Jesus, God will bring with Him those who have fallen asleep." The balance of the sentence seems to be against this view because it makes the verb "will bring" overweighted having a prepositional phrase before and after it which makes it almost impossible to see any difference between the two phrases. It is best to take the other possibility and connect "through Jesus" with "them also that are fallen asleep." This brings balance to the sentence as that "with him" naturally goes with "will bring." The acceptance of this view shows that "through Jesus" points to an effect accomplished by "the Jesus" mentioned in the first part of the verse. He removed the sting of death for His followers by His resurrection. There is therefore, no need to grieve since the promise of God bringing the dead with Him is clear and certain.

V:15 For this we say unto you by the word of the Lord,—A fuller explanation of the foregoing is introduced by the word "for" (Greek: *gar*). The demonstrative pronoun "this" refers to the following words of explanation beginning with "that we." The phrase "by the word of the Lord" refers to a word spoken by the historical Jesus. The word translated "by" is literally "in" (Greek: *en*) and makes the source clear. Was this a statement already recorded as words from Him? Some have sought such a statement in the gospels, but cannot find it. Matthew 24:31 most resembles it, but the differences are great. However, the most likely meaning of the statement is that it refers to some revelation given directly to Paul and, perhaps, to his co-workers (cf. Acts 18:9; Galatians 1:12; Ephesians 3:3). That all of the Lord's sayings are not recorded in the gospels is clear from Acts 20:35. The explanation is clear and it is correct because it comes from the Lord Himself.

that we that are alive, that are left unto the coming of the Lord,—"We that are alive" does not necessarily mean that Paul thought that he would be alive when the Lord came nor that Silvanus or Timothy would be. These men knew the uncertainty of life as well as we do. The words used by the writers may mean no more than "those Christians who are still living at the time of His coming." At times Paul associates himself with those who may be alive at the parousia (1 Corinthians 15:51,52 and here), at other times he associates himself with those who will be resurrected at that time (1 Corinthians 6:14; 2 Corinthians 4:14). It is true that the language here leaves room for the writers to be alive at His coming, but it also leaves room for their deaths before that time.

shall in no wise precede them that are fallen asleep.—The writers are not concerned with the time of the Lord's return but with what happens at the time He returns. The dead will miss nothing! The living will not go into the heavenly realm before, or without, the Christians who have died. The King James Version has the word "prevent" where the American Standard Version and other newer versions have "precede." In 1611 the English word "prevent" meant "come before" and was a good translation at the time.

V:16 For the Lord himself shall descend from heaven,—"For" is here from *hoti* and it introduces a more detailed positive statement on which the negative assurance of verse 15 is based. It is "the Lord himself" and not some deputy who will descend (cf. Acts 1:11; Mark 13:26; Luke 17:24). "From heaven" is from *apo ouranou*, the same phrase is in 2 Thessalonians

74

1:7 in reference to the Lord's coming. *Apo* ("from") is the appropriate word for referring to the visible heaven while *ek* ("out of") is the proper word for the invisible (cf. 1:10; 2 Corinthians 5:2). "Heaven" is singular and is a reference to the sky, the limit of vision upward (cf. Luke 2:15; Acts 1:11; 1 Peter 3:22).

with a shout,—Apparently this refers to a shout from the Lord as indicated by "his voice" in John 5:28,29. The word translated "shout" (Greek: *keleusma*) means shout of command or a command. It is not found elsewhere in the New Testament but is in the Greek Old Testament in Proverbs 30:27: "The locusts have no king, yet at the word of command they march in rank." F. F. Bruce gives several other examples of its use from secular Greek. The picture given here is the Lord leaving heaven at the end of this world system, giving His command, and immediately the spirits of the dead believers leave the realm of hades, and are reunited with their bodies which are raised from the grave as spiritual bodies.

with the voice of the archangel, and with the trump of God:—There is no doubt that the "shout" is different from the two sounds mentioned here. It comes from the Lord, these from a different source. Hendrikensen suggests that it is the archangel who sounds the trumpet. That view may be correct, but the more natural impression of the words is that there are three distinct sounds: the Lord's command, the voice of the archangel and the "trump of God." Only Jude 9 mentions an archangel specifically elsewhere in the New Testament where Michael is named. In Jewish tradition, there were seven archangels all given names, but no name is mentioned in this verse. The "trump" is evidently equated with the "last trump" of 1 Corinthians 15:52 in a similar context (cf. Matthew 24:31).

and the dead in Christ shall rise first;—The "dead in Christ" are those who had fallen asleep mentioned in verses 14 and 15. The fact that they are described as "in Christ" shows that the vital link made at their conversion does not end at physical death. Note that the dead here do not include the dead who died out of fellowship with God in Christ. The context is relating information about Christians, not pagans. That pagans will also be resurrected is clearly stated in John 5:28,29; Acts 24:15, but they are not included in this passage.

The words "shall rise" are from a future tense verb that refers to the resurrection from the grave. "First" (Greek: *proton*) is an adverb indicating an order of events; the following verse tells what will be next. Far from suffering any disadvantage at Christ's coming, the dead in Christ will, in a sense, actually have precedence over those in Christ who are still alive. Note that these words include all the Christian dead from the beginning to the second coming.

V:17 then we that are alive, that are left,—After the dead in Christ are raised, there "then" (Greek: *epeita*) follows the next stage in unraveling the story but the word does not indicate any interval between the two events. That there will be no interval is clear from 1 Corinthians 15:51,52, although the change is not mentioned here.

shall together with them be caught up in the clouds,—The words "together with them" shows that the two groups, the raised dead and the living, will "be caught up" as one company to meet the Lord. The two groups are completely equal in receiving the blessings promised. The verb "caught up" (Greek: *harapazo*) emphasizes the suddenness, the swiftness and the divine character of the event. It is God who takes them away. The English word "rapture" is often associated with this word based on the Latin word *rapturo* used in the Latin translation of this verse. "Rapture" has become the basis for a widely held view of the end time which has no basis in Scripture. The point of this verse is that at the coming of Christ, all faithful Christians, whether they have died or are still alive, will be taken to be with the Lord at the same time. Those who have died do not miss anything so there is no reason for the living to grieve. The catching away is described as "in the clouds." The "clouds" form the element with which those caught up are surrounded (cf. Acts 1:9).

to meet the Lord in the air:—The immediate purpose of the catching up is "to meet the Lord," literally "into a meeting with the Lord." The word translated "meet" certainly does at times refer to going out to meet some official and returning with him to his destination, but it may also refer to any meeting, friendly or hostile, and the context must determine what the writer meant. The meeting spoken of here is "in the air," literally "unto the air," apparently in the realm of the clouds. There is no reason to think that the caught up ones will come back to earth with the Lord since there is no evidence that He will come back to set foot on earth.

and so shall we ever be with the Lord.—The word "so" is from *houtos* which is an adverb of manner. It may be translated "in this way (manner), thus, so under these circumstances," and points to what has just been said to emphasize that all will be with the Lord forever. The place of that relationship with the Lord is undoubtedly heaven where Christ has gone to prepare a place for His people, and from whence He will come (cf. John 14:1-3; 2 Thessalonians 1:7).

V:18 Wherefore comfort one another with these words.—The words written and the arguments made should be enough to bring comfort, or cheer, or encouragement to those who were grieving. It is worth noting that an emotion (sorrow) may be displaced by teaching not primarily by another emotion. The Christian's intellect is the answer to un-Christian emotions.

Chapter 5

D. The certainty of Christ's coming, 5:1-11

V:1 But concerning the times and the seasons, brethren, ye have no need that aught be written unto you. V:2 For yourselves know perfectly that the day of the Lord so cometh as a thief in the night. V:3 When they are saying, Peace and safety, then sudden destruction cometh upon them, as travail upon a woman with child; and they shall in no wise escape. V:4 But ye, brethren, are not in darkness that that day should overtake you as a thief: V:5 for ye are all sons of light, and sons of the day: we are not of the night, nor of darkness; V:6 so then let us not sleep, as do the rest, but let us watch and be sober. V:7 For they that sleep sleep in the night; and they that are drunken are drunken in the night. V:8 But let us, since we are of the day, be sober, putting on the breastplate of faith and love; and for a helmet, the hope of salvation. V:9 For God appointed us not unto wrath, but unto the obtaining of salvation through our Lord Jesus Christ, V:10 who died for us, that, whether we wake or sleep, we should live together with him. V:11 Wherefore exhort one another, and build each other up, even as also ye do.

V:1 But concerning the times and the seasons, brethren,— The wording of this section shows that a new subject is introduced which is closely related to the section, 4:13-18. In that section the main point was what will happen to the dead in Christ at the parousia, here the point is time of His coming.

Two words are used here which refer to time. "Times" (Greek: *chronos*) is a common word for time, especially in the sense of duration. The English words "chronological" and "chronology" come from this Greek root and carry the same original intent. The second word is translated "seasons" (Greek: *kairos*).

Kairos is an interesting word. Delling shows that it has both a spatial and temporal sense in early Greek. It seems to be used only in the temporal sense in the New Testament (TDNT, 3:458-459). It refers to "the right moment," "the opportunity for doing, or avoiding to do, anything."

Several New Testament scholars hold the view that the two words are used to refer to different things: "times" to the period of time to elapse before the coming of the Lord, and "seasons" to what events will transpire before He comes (cf. Lightfoot, Morris, Lipscomb). There is some evidence, however, that the two words are intended to be synonymous in this verse. The use of two or more words when one would have been sufficient is not uncommon in the New Testament and is used for effect (cf. Marshall; Bruce, James Barr, *Biblical Words for Time*). This seems to be the best interpretation here.

ye have no need that aught be written unto you. — In 4:9 there was no need to write to those Christians about "love of the brethren" because they were taught of God to love, but here there is no need to write about "the times and the seasons" because they had already been taught in that area. There was a need to write about the relation of the parousia to the resurrection of the ones who die in Christ before it takes place, 4:13-18, but the matter of time setting had been covered.

V:2 For yourselves know perfectly — The point of verse one is repeated in a positive form here. The readers had received oral instruction about this subject. The word translated "yourselves" is emphatic. "You yourselves know" is a good translation. "Know" is the same word used several times already in this epistle (cf. 1:5; 2:1; 4:2). "Perfectly" (Greek: *akribos*) means "with exactness, accurately, precisely, well."

This means that the readers' knowledge in this matter was complete and needed no supplement.

that the day of the Lord so cometh as a thief in the night.—The fact that no one knows when the parousia will take place had been taught by Jesus Himself (Matthew 24:36-44; 25:13; Luke 12:39,40; cf. 2 Peter 3:10). The phrase "the day of the Lord" is an Old Testament concept. It referred to the day when the Lord would bring impartial judgment on sin and vindicate His name (Amos 5:18; Obadiah 15; Zephaniah 1:7ff.; Malachi 3:2; 4:5). The phrase is used in the New Testament where it is applied to Jesus Christ who is Lord (1 Corinthians 1:8; 5:5; Philippians 1:10; 2:16; 2 Peter 3:10). Sometimes it is referred to simply as "the day" or "that day" (cf. 1 Thessalonians 5:4; 2 Thessalonians 1:10; Hebrews 10:25). In the context of this verse, the phrase refers to the day of Christ's revelation in glory, when He comes to bring an end to this world system and to vindicate His people and judge the world in righteousness (Acts 17:31). The use of the present tense "cometh" instead of the future tense simply adds certainty to the fact of His coming. "As a thief" is used several times in statements about Jesus' coming as is mentioned above. The point in each place is that the time for His coming is known only to God. Therefore, Christians need to be ready every day lest He come when they are not prepared.

The warning given here is appropriate for today. Those first readers were to be careful not to get involved in schemes for setting dates for God's actions. Jesus warned of the danger earlier, now Paul and his co-workers join in that warning and all need to heed it. This matter is important because it is so easy to get caught up in speculations about when things will happen that we forget about the need to live for Christ now! This is a recurring theme in the Thessalonian epistles.

V:3 When they are saying, Peace and safety, then sudden destruction cometh upon them,—After urging the Christians to be constantly prepared for the parousia, the writers turn to the unbelieving world. The opening words of this verse make it clear that no specific time is intended. "When" (Greek: *hotan*) followed by a present subjunctive verb means "whenever they may say." "Peace and safety" reminds one of the warnings given by the Old Testament prophets like Jeremiah (6:14; 8:11) and Ezekiel (13:10). It is more likely, however, that the writers of this text were influenced by Jesus' own teaching in passages like Luke 21:34-36. God's judgment, the day of the Lord, will come suddenly upon all inhabitants of the entire earth, including unwatchful disciples. The emphasis here is more on those of the world who think nothing can happen to them (cf. 2 Peter 3:3ff.).

The word "destruction" (Greek: *olethros*) is used in the Greek Old Testament where it often has the meaning of an eschatological destruction as a result of God's judgment (cf. Jeremiah 5:6; 22:7; Ezekiel 6:14). In the New Testament the word is found four times, all in Paul's writings. In each of the places it refers to the ultimate fate of sinners except in 1 Corinthians 5:5 (see also 2 Thessalonians 1:9; 1 Timothy 6:9). In the 1 Corinthians passage, it seems to refer to the expulsion of one from the church fellowship with the expectation that he would repent. All who are unprepared are included in the word "them." It should be noted that this word does not mean the destruction of being, but of well being with the result that the thing, or person, destroyed cannot accomplish its intended purpose.

as travail upon a woman with child; — Adding to the figure of the thief suggesting the unexpected nature of the parousia, this phrase suggests the inevitability of it. The word "travail" or "birth pain" (Greek: *odin*) is a common figure for intense pain and sorrow and comes from the Old Testament (cf. Jeremiah 4:31; Hosea 13:13; Micah 4:9). Note that there is no time indicated in the sentence and, as is clear elsewhere, Paul did not know when the parousia would take place (see 4:14).

and they shall in no wise escape. — This very strong negative statement makes it very clear that men cannot escape the coming judgment. It is interesting that the same strong negative is used in 4:15 to emphasize that the living Christians will have no advantage over the dead ones. This lesson still needs to be emphasized: there are no other alternatives beside life in Christ or eternal loss (cf. John 5:28,29).

V:4 But ye, brethren, are not in darkness, that that day should overtake you as a thief:—"But ye, brethren" sets the believers in contrast with those mentioned in verse 3, the unbelievers caught unprepared for the day of the Lord. The personal pronoun "ye" (Greek: *humeis*) is placed so that it is to be emphasized and sharpens the contrast as does the direct address, "brethren."

The Thessalonian Christians, in contrast to those who are unprepared, are now discussed at length. First, they are described negatively as "not in darkness." "Darkness" is a common word to describe those in an unsaved condition. Ignorance of God and His will is darkness and can only be replaced by revelation from God which was provided through the apostles for believers in Thessalonica.

The first "that" in the text is from *hina* a word which normally introduces either a purpose or result clause. Here it indicates contemplated result rather than purpose. Unbelievers will be overtaken, but not these Christians. The words "that day" are literally "the day" and refer to the day of the Lord mentioned in verse 2. Those who live in the light will not be found unprepared for the coming of the Lord. It should be noted that a few important manuscripts of 1 Thessalonians have "like thieves" and the words are in the accusative case. This wording compares the unprepared with thieves who are overtaken by the dawn. The reading of the singular "like a thief" in the nominative is the best reading as in our text.

V:5 for ye are all sons of light, and sons of day:—After asserting that the Christians should not be overtaken by darkness (vs. 4), the writers give a reason for their statement. By saying that they are "sons of light" indicates that "light" is their distinguishing characteristic. For similar thoughts see Luke 16:8; John 12:36; Ephesians 5:8 and notice the antithesis of light and darkness in John's writings. "Sons of day" is a synonym of "sons of light." Believers already are citizens of heaven (Philippians 3:20) and their lives should be lived in such a way that they demonstrate that citizenship. There is apparently a reference here to the day of the Lord. Christians live in anticipation of that day.

we are not of the night, nor of darkness:—The change from "ye" to "we" makes the point more comprehensive (cf. 4:4,7 for a similar change). The duties stated have application to all Christians not just those of Thessalonica. The genitives "night" and "darkness" are evidently descriptive words and are essentially synonyms. Note the use of the present tense verb which shows that Christians are to always live in the light.

V:6 so then let us not sleep, as do the rest,—"So then" (Greek: *ara oun*) is a common phrase in Paul to introduce a further step in an argument or in summing up a point. In this place it marks the transition to direct exhortation. Since "we are sons of light," we are exhorted to be watchful. The words "let us not sleep" have the very words of Christ for their basis. He said, "If the master of the house had known in what hour the thief was coming, he would have watched, and not have left his house to be broken through" (Luke 12:39; cf. the warning in Mark 13:35,36). The word for "sleep" here is *katheudo* and is not the same word as in 4:13. This word is used of death only in Matthew 9:24 and the parallel passages, Mark 5:39 and Luke 8:52. It is used of natural sleep several times, but here and in three other places it indicates worldly indifference to spiritual matters on the part of believers (vs. 10; Mark 13:36; Ephesians 5:14). "As do the rest" was used in 4:13 in speaking of those without hope. Here the phrase refers to the remainder of humanity, that is, those who are unbelievers. Those are in the area of darkness, being insensitive to spiritual matters, and still have a sense of security.

but let us watch and be sober.—"Watch" (Greek: *gregoreo*) is used of mental alertness which is the opposite of sleep. The word is used of the intentness of the mind set on getting instruction, looking for the answer to prayer, for the Lord's return and for vigilance in opposing Satan and false teachers as well as in carrying out a purpose. It is used in this place of vigilance against spiritual dangers of any type. "Sober" (Greek: *nepho*) may mean to be sober in the sense that one is not under the influence of strong drink, but here it points to a condition of stability of character or of self-control (cf. 2 Peter 5:8).

V:7 For they that sleep sleep in the night;—The writers seem to be making a play on words. "Sleep" is an appropriate action for night time, but the point here is that those who are of the darkness or night are acting appropriately for their spiritual condition. The wicked and careless are children of the night and live in spiritual darkness. The warning is to be on guard against falling into the many spiritual traps laid down by Satan.

and they that are drunken are drunken at night.—Another experience from ordinary life is used. Sleep and drunkenness usually occur at night. Both Jews and pagans considered it disgraceful for one to be drunk in the daytime (cf. Acts 2:13-15; 2 Peter 2:13). Activities stemming from drunkenness are expected among nonbelievers but Christians are to avoid such things.

V:8 But let us, since we are of the day, be sober,—The need to be "sober" is emphasized again. The personal pronoun "us" is emphatic to make clear the difference between those of the world and Christians. "Sober" is the same word used in verse 6 and has the same meaning of stability and self-control so that one would avoid all kinds of excess.

putting on the breastplate of faith and love;—The foregoing reminds the authors that the Christian is a soldier. Paul often uses language that makes this analogy. The Christian has "put on Christ" (Galatians 3:26,27) and is urged to put on "as God's elect,. . .a heart of compassion, kindness, lowliness, meekness, longsuffering" (Colossians 3:12). These words describe "the new man" who has been created after God's likeness (Ephesians 4:24). However, the Christian is a soldier and must wear the armor provided for him by God. A more complete list of the armor is provided in Ephesians 6:11-17, but here only defensive armor is mentioned. "The breastplate" is explained by the words "of faith and love." Faith is the proper attitude of the Christian toward God and love his proper attitude toward his fellow saints.

and for a helmet, the hope of salvation.—Another part of the armor which is defensive in function is mentioned. It seems that, in this context, the writers are urging the readers to defend themselves against being unprepared so that the day of the Lord will not come upon them as a thief. These two defensive items have allowed the writers to bring up the triad of faith, hope and love again (cf. 1:3). These are very important to the Christian's defense against Satan's power of temptation. "Hope" includes the concepts of desire plus expectation, and is a powerful motive to faithfulness. "Salvation" has been given to the Christian but its completion is still future, thus hope is the proper word.

V:9 For God appointed us not unto wrath,—The opening word of verse 9 literally means "because" (Greek: *hoti*) and introduces the reason for the statement in verse 8. God's people need to be sober and self-controlled and should protect themselves with the armor supplied. God "appointed" (Greek: *tithemi*) believers to be of service to Himself as the middle voice indicates. God did not intend for humans to live their lives on this earth only to receive wrath. "Wrath" evidently refers to an eternal separation from God.

The use of the word "appointed" does not give support for the widely held view that men's eternal destiny was arbitrarily predetermined in the past without regard for the actions of each individual. God has always acted in ways that are designed to bring sinful people to repentance. He does not wish anyone to be lost (2 Peter 3:9), but, in fact, He wants all to be saved (1 Timothy 2:4). That same wish is expressed in the next clause.

but unto the obtaining of salvation through our Lord Jesus Christ,—The word "but" (Greek: *alla*) indicates a strong contrast: not wrath but obtaining salvation. The word translated "obtaining" has to do with an acquisition of something, here it is salvation. This verse does not simply say that God has appointed Christians for salvation, but the writers want to make it clear that the believers have to play their part in the process. Marshall says, "One might say that God's plan is that the readers should do what is necessary to acquire salvation" (139). God's plan for saving sinful man includes man meeting his responsibilities (cf. Romans 2:6-11; 2 Corinthians 5:10; Colossians 3:24,25). If the Thessalonian Christians obtain the salvation offered by God, they must remain spiritually alert and continue to be clothed with the armor just mentioned in verse 8. If the eternal destiny of these readers was already set, such warnings and admonitions are meaningless.

"Salvation" is mentioned in both verses 8 and 9 and evidently includes all the blessings of the gospel whether in this life in Christ or future life with Him in eternity. The emphasis is on the latter aspect of life. "Salvation" is available through Jesus Christ and no other (cf. John 14:6; Acts 4:12).

V:10 who died for us,—The means of salvation was completed in Jesus' death for us. The implication is that if He had not died for us we would be appointed to wrath. No explanation of how the event affected the destiny of believers is given here. The teaching about the cross and redemption is expounded in places like Romans 3:24-26 and 2 Corinthians 5:19-21. These passages make it clear that His death had the force of an atoning sacrifice for sin. Jesus' sacrifice provided for the salvation of all people (Hebrews 2:9), but only those who, on the basis of their faith, accept the salvation provided actually partake of its blessings.

that, whether we wake or sleep, we should live together with him.—Christ's death is so sufficient that it brings assurance of future life with all obstacles removed. The words "wake or sleep" are used to refer to those who are living and those who are dead at the parousia. There is no reason to think that these words are referring to moral watchfulness and carelessness, as in verse 6. Paul and the other writers would not say that it makes little or no difference whether one lives like sons of light or sons of darkness. Lifestyle does make a difference. The point is that whether one is still alive or has already died a physical death his fellowship with God continues as is made clear in 4:13-18.

V:11 Wherefore exhort one another,—"Wherefore" introduces the conclusion of this section of the epistle, 5:1-11. The point is about the same as 4:18 which closes the previous section. Since that section is concerned with a need for comfort and this one with duties and dangers which call for vigilance, this is a little more comprehensive. "Exhort one another" may be translated "comfort one another." The use of the present tense verb indicates that the exhorting is to be done continually. All Christians need encouragement which is based on God's truth revealed in Scripture.

and build each other up, even as also ye do.—This part of the verse is closely related to the first part. To build up refers to the promotion of spiritual growth. One can build up another by teaching and by example. Those in Thessalonica were doing those things already, but they needed to be encouraged to continue lest some grow slack.

V. GENERAL EXHORTATIONS, 5:12-22

A. Appeal for harmony among the Christians, 5:12-15

V:12 We beseech you, brethren, to know them that labor among you, and are over you in the Lord, and admonish you; V:13 and to esteem them exceedingly highly in love for their work's sake. Be at peace among yourselves. V:14 And we exhort you, brethren, admonish the disorderly, encourage the fainthearted, support the weak, be longsuffering toward all. V:15 See that none render unto any one evil for evil; but always follow after that which is good, one toward another, and toward all.

V:12 But we beseech you, brethren, to know them that labor among you, and are over you in the Lord, and admonish you;— Clearly a new section begins here. Evidently there were some internal problems in the congregation and these practical instructions are designed to settle those matters. The word "beseech" is a word that means simply "to request" something (see 4:1) and is directed to all the "brethren" in this congregation. "To know" is from *oida* and includes knowledge as well as coming to a full understanding of the true character and word of those described in the three participle phrases which follow.

The grammatical structure makes it clear that the three phrases are describing one group of people. They are the ones "that labor" among the members of the congregation. "Labor" is from a verb that means "to grow weary, to work with effort" and it may refer to either bodily or mental labor. The noun form of this word is used in 1:3 in reference to the hard labor which expresses love. The word is very general and the precise nature of the work is undetermined.

"And are over you" is another participle phrase referring to the same people as the phrase "that labor among you." The verb itself (Greek: *proistemi*) combines the thoughts of leading, protecting and caring for. The word has often been given some official meaning and made to describe the elders. Of course, elders may be included here because of their responsibilities, but it is not certain that they are meant here. No one knows if the church in Thessalonica had elders at the time of the writing of this epistle. The wording of the text can equally be applied to influential teachers or preachers or, more likely in view of verse 20, prophets. Whoever they were, they were providing leadership by their teaching and caring service among the Thessalonians "in the Lord."

and admonish you;—The word translated "admonish" is found only in Paul's writings and once in Acts where Paul's speech is being reported (Acts 20:21). It involves attaching some blame to the admonished but it is done so in kindness and tenderness. It certainly would fit the work of teachers who really care for their fellow Christians.

The grammatical structure of this verse not only indicates one group of people, it implies that the "labor" is defined by the two following phrases, "are over you in the Lord" and "admonish you."

V:13 and to esteem them exceedingly highly in love for their work's sake.—Those who labor among them are to be held in "esteem," a word which means here "to believe, consider, or think" (Greek: *hegeomai*) about those men "exceedingly highly" (Greek *huperekperrissos*). The thinking about these workers is not to be based on personality, wealth or those things which people often notice. The esteem is to be "in love" and "because of their work." The important thing was that the service should be done, and that those who do it receive affectionate recognition and gratitude with the spirit of Jesus (cf. Luke 22:24-27; 1 Corinthians 16:15,16).

Be at peace among yourselves.—These words indicate that peace prevailed among the first readers and that they should make every reasonable effort to maintain that peace. There is no necessity to think there was trouble already in the congregation, but that is not an impossible motive for these words. Jesus taught His disciples to "be at peace with one another" (Mark 9:50), and Paul admonished other Christians with similar words (Romans 12:18; 2 Corinthians 13:11). All Christians should seek to have peace with all other Christians.

V:14 And we exhort you, brethren,—The same group addressed in verse 12 is addressed here. The writers "exhort" (Greek: *parakaleo*) the "brethren," evidently all the "brethren" in Thessalonica are included. It has been argued that these words are addressed to those who "are over you in the Lord" (verse 12). There is, however, nothing in the text itself to suggest that. Such a change could be signaled by body movement or tone change if the speaker was present, but in writing it would have to be indicated by a word or words. It is true that the types of service mentioned in the following words are a responsibility of elders and leaders, but not exclusively theirs. All members of the congregation have these responsibilities (cf. verse 11).

admonish the disorderly,—The instructions in this verse move on to proper treatment of those people with special problems. The first special group is the "disorderly" (Greek: *ataktos*). This word was primarily a military term describing a soldier who was out of step or out of rank. It came to be used in reference to almost anything which was out of order. Most commentaries suggest that the word here refers to the idleness among the Christians which had been brought about by a misunderstanding about Christ's coming. Frame (197) shows that the word does not refer to legitimate leisure, but to loafing. Such folk need to be admonished (see verse 12).

encourage the fainthearted,—The second special group is the "fainthearted." The word so translated (Greek: *oligopsuchos*) is found only here in the New Testament and literally means "small-souled," but indicates the despondent or discouraged or fearful. Such need to be encouraged, that is, treated with tender concern, consoled and made to feel as if he counts.

support the weak,—The "weak" is the third group. "Support" implies that these need help and to be cared for. The caution is here not to turn away from the weak. "Weak" could refer to physical weakness or illness, but the context shows that the weakness is in faith. It would also include lack of courage or spiritual insight. These would be in danger of falling away from the faith, thus the need for support.

be longsuffering toward all.—The last of the injunctions is to be "longsuffering" or "patient." The word used (Greek: *makrothumeo*) literally means "long-tempered" and indicates a willingness to put up with people and their awkwardness and even opposition to the one trying to help. The word means that one shows restraint toward people who deserve punishment. This is a characteristic that all need to develop and demonstrate to other Christians and to all people.

V:15 See that none render unto any one evil for evil;—The word "see" points to the need for attention to what was happening in daily matters. No one should be allowed to be overtaken by the temptation to "get even." The entire congregation has a responsibility for the conduct of its individual members. The wording may indicate that each one is to watch over himself, but it seems to have a broader application. This is basic Christian teaching and is evidently rooted in Jesus' teaching (Matthew 5:44-48; cf. Hebrews 12:15). "Render" means "to give back, pay back" and indicates the modern idea "to get even." "Evil" is what causes injury or works mischief of any kind. The word translated "for" actually means "in exchange for" or "in return for" in this passage.

but always follow after that which is good, one toward another, and toward all.—The Christian is not to seek to "get even" with those who do him wrong. Instead he is to "always follow after" the good. "Always" shows that the rule being laid down had no exceptions. "Follow after" (Greek: *dioko*) has the idea of "pursuing earnestly." The word has in it the concept of earnestness with which one should pursue the object set before him. The word "good" refers to acts of love which will be helpful to those to whom they are done. The word covers a wide range of things, and the use of the present tense shows that it is to be the habitual attitude of the Christian (cf. Romans 12:17; 1 Peter 3:9). The attitude is to be expressed toward fellow-Christians and to all people. Nonretaliation for personal wrongs may well be the best evidence of personal Christian maturity.

V:16 Rejoice always;—Following the commands in verses 12-15 is impossible without a close personal relationship with God. Because of that, the writers turn to the Christian's inner life. The word "rejoice" is a present tense indicating that the attitude should continue to be one of rejoicing. "Always" emphasizes that there should be no interruption in the matter.

V:17 pray without ceasing;—"Pray" is a comprehensive word and includes the other words for prayer in the New Testament whether individual or congregational prayer is meant. One who understands his own weakness, his inability and his utter dependence on God cannot refrain from asking for help. "Without ceasing" indicates that one should constantly be in an attitude of prayer. Of course, one cannot be continually saying words in prayer, but he can have an attitude of prayer. A study of Jesus' prayer life will demonstrate that He is our example (cf. Luke 3:21; 5:16; 6:12; 9:18,28-29; 10:21-22; 11:1; 22:41-45; 23:46). Paul is also a good example and clearly shows that prayer may be short and spontaneous under all circumstances (cf. Ephesians 6:18; Colossians 4:2; 1 Thessalonians 3:11-13; 5:23; 2 Thessalonians 1:11; 2:16; 3:5,16). The maintenance of spiritual life depends upon continuing in prayer.

V:18 in everything give thanks;—The child of God is to give thanks for everything and under all circumstances whether things are good (1 Thessalonians 1:2-5), during persecution (James 1:2-4), in times of sorrow or adversity (cf. Philippians

91

4:6,10-12). Thanksgiving is a type of prayer and thanksgiving under all types of circumstances was characteristic of Jesus.

for this is the will of God in Christ Jesus to you-ward.—In 4:3 the will of God is the sanctification of His people which is an all inclusive concept in scope as is demonstrated in 4:3-8 and in 5:23. In this verse the sanctifying work of the Spirit within the Christian is expressed in rejoicing, prayer and thanksgiving. "God's will in Christ Jesus" may be paraphrased as "God's will for you as members of the Christian fellowship" (Bruce). Much the same point is made in Philippians 2:12,13.

V:19 Quench not the Spirit;—The use of the present imperative with the negative *me* could mean that the readers were quenching the Spirit and that they should stop doing so. The context, however, seems to indicate that they must constantly refrain from quenching the Spirit.

The verb "quench" (Greek: *sbennumi*) literally means to put out a fire and is so used in Matthew 12:20 and Hebrews 11:34. It is used in a metaphorical sense in places like Mark 9:48 and Ephesians 6:16. Here the reference seems to be to the association of the Spirit with fire (cf. Romans 12:11f; 2 Timothy 1:6). There was evidently a tendency in the church in Thessalonica to quench the "fire" or influence of the Spirit. If that is correct, it indicates a reaction against what appeared to be an overenthusiastic emphasis on the Spirit which is the opposite of those in Corinth (cf. 1 Corinthians 12-14).

It is possible that Paul and his co-workers were speaking of the promised indwelling of the Spirit in each Christian. The Spirit is compared to a fire within, but some were evidently restraining His influence. However, the context indicates that spiritual gifts are the subject being considered. The writers pick out one specific example which is the matter of prophecy. This example was chosen because it was considered to be the most important (1 Corinthians 14:1-3). All the spiritual gifts were for the advantage of the church, but in this congregation were being quenched.

V:20 despise not prophesyings;—This seems to be the one specific example of quenching the Spirit in verse 19. "Despise" (Greek: *exoutheneo*) means to consider as nothing, to downgrade or to set down as of no account. The prophet is a spokesman for God. When the prophet speaks he is to be heard and obeyed, not ignored. It may also be that some with the prophetic gift were not using it since the prophet could control the Spirit in such cases (1 Corinthians 14:29-33).

The application of verses 19 and 20 in the church today is that since the miraculous gifts of the Spirit are no longer in vogue, the work of the Spirit may be rejected or ignored so that the benefits are missed. The prophetic message recorded in Scripture may be despised and the end result will be an eternal separation from God and His glory.

V:21 prove all things; — Some in the first century as in the centuries following have attempted to imitate prophecy. It was, and is, important that such imitations be detected and rejected. No criteria are given here for proving or testing the prophets, but consistency with other known revelation would be one method (cf. 1 Corinthians 14:29; 1 John 4:1-3). Of course, all teaching should be tested by God's revelation. The word used here is *dokimazo* and means to approve after testing.

hold fast that which is good; —"Hold fast" more literally means to lay hold of, to take possession of something. The point here is that after testing a thing to learn if it is genuine, one should take it and make it a part of his faith and life. The words "that which is good," in the context, refers to the word of prophecy which after being tested proves to be from God. There is an implication that if the thing tested does not prove to be genuine, it should be rejected.

V:22 abstain from every form of evil.—"Abstain" means to hold one's self from. The point is emphasized — if a word of prophecy is not approved, the Christian must not hold it. The principle is broader than words claiming to be prophecy and includes all teaching. "Every form" is from a word that means visible form, that which can be seen, or it may refer possibly to kind or species or class. "Of evil" is best taken as describing the false prophecy no matter what its form. Consider Jesus' warning as you consider this context (Matthew 7:15; cf. 2 Corinthians 11:13-15). This explanation of the verse does not detract from statements elsewhere in which other things are to be avoided (cf. 4:3).

VI. Conclusion, 5:23-28

V:23 And the God of peace himself sanctify you wholly; and may your spirit and soul and body be preserved entire, without blame at the coming of our Lord Jesus Christ. V:24 Faithful is he that calleth you, who will also do it. V:25 Brethren, pray for us. V:26 Salute all the brethren with a holy kiss. V:27 I adjure you by the Lord that this epistle be read unto all the brethren. V:28 The grace of our Lord Jesus Christ be with you.

Verses 23 and 24 are a prayer concluding the exhortations of the previous section. These words include the entire fellowship and give an assurance that God will fulfill the request (cf. 3:11-13).

V:23 And the God of peace himself sanctify you wholly;— No matter how the readers may be taught and urged to be faithful, they cannot do so apart from God. God is the one from whom peace comes (cf. Romans 15:33; 16:20; Philippians 4:9; Hebrews 13:20 for the same thought). The entire range of gospel blessings may be summed up by the word "peace," and God is the source of them all. "Sanctify" is from an aorist tense verb and here refers to the completion of the process of sanctification which is progressive through the Christian life. In 4:3,4,7 the importance of sanctification in matters of sexual purity are shown, here the appeal is to all areas of life. "Wholly" (Greek: *holoteles*) is found only here in the New Testament. The word means "entirely" and includes the future idea of completion (Lightfoot).

and may your spirit and soul and body be preserved entire, without blame—This is another way of expressing the desire for complete sanctification of the readers. The use of the aorist tense verb again points to the completion of the process of sanctification and salvation. The word "entire" emphasizes the desire for the entire person of the readers to be kept blameless, that is, that each will be kept so that nothing blameworthy will be attached to him.

94

It is beyond the scope of a brief commentary to discuss the Biblical Doctrine of Man. It is sufficient here to say that the use of the three nouns, spirit, soul and body, is to give more emphasis to the completeness of the sanctification for which the writers pray. The statement means something like: "May every part of your being be kept entirely without fault."

at the coming of our Lord Jesus Christ.—Note the close parallels in the prayer in 3:11-13 and this one. In both the writers pray that the converts in Thessalonica may be preserved entirely without fault until the Lord comes and that they will be found in that pure condition at His coming at which time they will be perfected in holiness.

V:24 Faithful is he that calleth you,—Even though the prayer may be expressed as a wish (indicated by the use of the optative mood), there is no lack of confidence that what is asked will be done. God is "faithful;" He can be depended on! He is the one "that calleth you." The present tense verb may indicate that God's call is constantly being heard by His people. The word may also mean that God is constantly calling men to Himself if they will but hear. The latter seems best. Either way, God's concern is clear.

who will also do it.—God is a doer. He will perform what He has promised. He will sanctify and He will keep them if they will follow the instructions given. God's keeping of one depends upon that one's willingness to be kept and the keeping of himself in the love of God (Jude 21). Any failure will be man's fault, not God's.

V:25 Brethren, pray for us.—The request to be remembered by those for whom he has prayed is rather common in Paul's writings (Romans 15:30; 2 Corinthians 1:11; Ephesians 6:19; Colossians 4:3; 2 Thessalonians 3:1). The verb is the present tense showing that they are asking for the continued prayers of the readers.

V:26 Salute all the brethren with a holy kiss.—Almost the same command is given in Romans 16:16; 1 Corinthians 16:20; and 2 Corinthians 13:12. Peter used a similar phrase when he said, "Salute one another with a kiss of love" (1 Peter 5:14). In the first century "greeting one another," or "saluting one another" with a kiss was a well-established practice before Christianity (Kelcy). The "holy kiss" signified the bond that united the people in a holy fellowship. Later (early fourth century) it was stated that at the Lord's Supper "the men are to give one another the kiss in the Lord and the women likewise to one another" (*Apostolic Constitutions* 2.57.17). In this verse, there is a slight emphasis on "all the brethren." Following this practice would help in quieting any tension among the readers. No individual is to be left out, even those who have been rebuked for loafing or those who are weak are included.

V:27 I adjure you by the Lord that this epistle be read unto all the brethren.—The change from the plural to the singular indicates that this statement is from Paul himself. The emphasis is still on the phrase "all the brethren." The word translated "I adjure" is used only here in the New Testament. Its use shows that the author wanted the readers to consider this injunction important. In fact, the words put the readers under oath that no one, nor any group, will be left out so that the epistle is not read to them. The word "read" almost certainly means to read aloud. The phrase "by the Lord" adds emphasis to the statement and makes it clear that the Lord is the person invoked in the oath.

Paul's words do not imply that he was unaware of, or that he ignored, the ban on oaths spoken by Jesus (Matthew 5:34). The words in this passage do not attempt to strengthen a statement of Paul's own by invoking the divine name, but these words are an appeal to the readers to act in this matter as responsible to the Lord Himself.

V:28 The grace of our Lord Jesus Christ be with you.—"Grace" was a part of the introductory greeting in 1:1 and as is Paul's custom, grace is picked up again in the final words of the epistle. The language could be formal, but here it takes the readers to the heart of the gospel, to the person of Jesus Christ who is Lord and the source of all spiritual blessings.

The love of the apostle for the Christians in Thessalonica is clear, especially in these last verses. May each one, as God's person, follow not only the principles of command in this letter but the example of genuine love demonstrated in this epistle.

Introduction to 2 Thessalonians

Most of what was said in the introduction to 1 Thessalonians applies to the second epistle. There are some matters which need to be mentioned because the second epistle has been more widely disputed than the first.

The Authenticity of 2 Thessalonians

The external evidence for the authenticity of 2 Thessalonians is earlier and stronger than for 1 Thessalonians. It is quoted more often by early writers than is the first epistle. The passage about "the man of sin" (2:1-12) evidently made a strong impression on those early writers since frequent reference is made to it. Although Polycarp evidently makes reference to 2 Thessalonians as does Justin Martyr, Irenaeus is apparently the first to mention it by name. Clement of Alexandria and Tertullian both quote it as from Paul. This epistle is in the Muratorian Canon, the Syriac, the Vulgate and the Old Latin Versions. It is also in the canon of Marcion. It is in every later list of New Testament books. This epistle was known and accepted in every section of the Christian world.

The internal evidence for this epistle being from Paul is also very strong. In two different places the author refers to himself as Paul (1:1; 3:17). Of course, Silvanus and Timothy are joined with Paul as authors, but Paul is basically responsible for the writing. The thought is Paul's beyond doubt. William

Neil wrote, "In respect of vocabulary, style, and fundamental theological assumptions, the second letter is as Pauline as the first" (xxi).

The evidence for the epistle is strong and reasonable. The early church accepted 2 Thessalonians as a genuine work of Paul. Yet the internal evidence has been used by some to argue that the traditional conclusion is improbable. There are basically four grounds for objecting to the older conclusions although some divide them into more.

1. Eschatology. It is claimed that there is a marked difference in the view of the parousia in 1 Thessalonians and in 2 Thessalonians. In the first epistle, the parousia is imminent (4:14-5:3), but in the second the author denies this and says that the "falling away" and the revelation of "the man of sin" must occur first (2:1-12). Some critics suggest that the section about "the man of sin" was added to a genuine Pauline letter some time later. This suggestion is based on the supposition that "the man of sin" was to be identified with the thought that Nero had not actually died and that he was going to reappear as the great enemy of Christianity. That theory developed later than the date of 2 Thessalonians and could not have been a part of the original work. Such a view is almost totally rejected by modern writers. The reason is that 1 Thessalonians 5:1-11 shows that the missionaries had already taught about the uncertainty of the time for the parousia (cf. 2 Thessalonians 2:5). It is true that there is no parallel to "the man of sin" in the first epistle, but it does not follow that the same writers could not have written both epistles. Second Thessalonians 2:5 shows clearly that the teaching is not new to the readers. It is safe to conclude that no real problem exists because the two epistles confront different questions about Christ's coming.

2. A change of audience. It seems clear from 1 Thessalonians that the audience is basically Gentile. Since the second epistle assumes a greater knowledge of the Old Testament (1:6-10; 2:1-12), it is thought that it is addressed to a Jewish audience. There are, however, no references to anything in the second epistle that Gentiles could not have known. The sermons in

Acts demonstrate a strong awareness of Old Testament teaching in the early preaching, even to Gentiles. If Mark was written to a Gentile audience as is generally thought, the apocalyptic element was not unintelligible to Gentiles. This seems especially true since the writers had already spoken to them of "these things" (2:5).

3. **Change of tone and style.** In more recent years the critics have shifted their emphasis to the literary relationship between the two epistles. It is claimed that 2 Thessalonians is more formal and frigid than the first epistle. The first is characterized by a warmth and glowing affection toward the readers while the second is described as chilly and officially formal. The charge of formality in 2 Thessalonians is based mostly on the use of a few phrases like "we are bound to give thanks" (1:3; 2:13), and "we command you" (3:6,12), while 1 Thessalonians has expressions like "we give thanks" (1:2) and "our exhortation" (2:3). Notice, however, that 2 Thessalonians has a number of warm, personal statements also (1:11; 2:16,17; 3:3-5). The change of tone and/or style is easily accounted for because of a change of circumstances which brought about a change of mood.

4. **The similarities.** Some ask why Paul and his co-workers would have written two epistles so close in time on the same basic subject matter. They ask, "Would they have repeated themselves so much?" A. C. McGiffert suggests that about one third of 2 Thessalonians is "more or less a close reproduction of the first epistle" (*Encyclopedia Biblica*, iv, col. 5044). There are some agreements, but Frame (49) demonstrates that they are not long and that the similarity of wording often occurs in different settings in the two epistles. Every one of the differences and similarities can be accounted for by considering the situation in Thessalonica at the time of writing.

All these objections have been adequately answered in the many good Introductions to the New Testament available and in the various commentaries. Several of these are listed in the Bibliography.

Another matter to consider briefly is the proposal that 2 Thessalonians was actually written before 1 Thessalonians. This was proposed as early as 1641 by Hugo Grotius. Others have followed him and developed the argument more. The major arguments are: (1) 1 Thessalonians was placed first in the New Testament only because it was longer; (2) Timothy would naturally take a letter with him as he was sent to Thessalonica; (3) the distress indicated in 2 Thessalonians is in the present, but in 1 Thessalonians it is in the past; (4) some of the warnings in the first epistle make sense only if they are based on the second epistle (cf. 1 Thessalonians 4:10,12 and 2 Thessalonians 3:6ff.); (5) the mention of the personal signature in 2 Thessalonians 3:17 makes sense only if it is the first written; (6) the statement that there is no need for instructions about "the times and the seasons" (1 Thessalonians 5:1) makes better sense if the readers were already acquainted with 2 Thessalonians 2:3ff.

All of these points have been adequately discussed in the Introductions and commentaries available. The conclusion is that there is no valid argument, or group of arguments, that seriously challenge the authenticity of 2 Thessalonians or the traditional order of the New Testament books.

The Occasion for 2 Thessalonians

The immediate motive for writing this epistle was no doubt a report received by Paul and his co-workers about conditions in Thessalonica. There is no available information about who delivered the news, but it is clear that he was aware of the response to the first epistle as well as to additional matters, especially about the second coming. Some of the information needed a response so no time would be wasted in getting the second epistle written and sent.

There was some good response to the first epistle mentioned in this second one: they had made progress in their faith (1:3) and had remained stedfast under persecution (1:4); they had apparently had the distress about the dead loved ones relieved by the comments in the first epistle. On the other hand, new tensions connected with the second coming are evident (2:2ff.). Apparently a letter claiming to be from Paul, or some person claiming divine inspiration, had caused these misunderstandings. It is made clear that the coming had not yet occurred and there was no need to stop working at their occupations. The leisure time had led some to a point of being "disorderly" and/or "busybodies," interfering in other people's lives (3:10-12). These are some of the things which gave an occasion for the epistle.

Place and Date of Writing

Paul, Silvanus, and Timothy were still together at the time this letter was written as is clear from 1:1. After the time of ministry in Corinth (Acts 18), there is no additional information about Silvanus in the book of Acts after 18:5. Timothy was with Paul in Ephesus (Acts 19:22), but all three seem not to have been together at any time after Corinth. Since 2 Thessalonians presents conditions in the church which are the same as in 1 Thessalonians, the conclusion is that this second epistle was written from Corinth as was the first.

It is not possible for a long time to have passed between the writing of the two epistles. A few months is the most possible, perhaps three months are sufficient. The first epistle was dated in the spring of A.D. 51 and the second should be dated a few months later in the same year.

The Teaching in 2 Thessalonians

The teachings in 1 Thessalonians are essentially found in 2 Thessalonians also. Note the comments on the first epistle.

God. A similar emphasis on God is in both epistles. In 2 Thessalonians, God is the one to whom thanks should be directed (1:3; 2:13); He is the source of peace, grace, and love (1:2,12; 3:5); they pointed to Him as the source of comfort and hope (2:16,17); He chose the readers for salvation (2:13); He counts them as worthy (1:11); He is the one who judges righteously (1:5).

Christ. The high view of Christ's nature is continued in the second epistle (1:1,2,12). Christ is described by the term "Lord" no fewer than 12 times in this epistle. He is included with the Father in prayer for comfort and strength (2:16,17). Christ will be revealed at the judgment when He will render vengeance upon those who do not obey Him (1:7,8). He is the basis for the charges given to the readers (3:6,12).

The Holy Spirit. Apparently the Holy Spirit is mentioned only one time in 2 Thessalonians. The Spirit works in sanctification along with belief of the truth (2:13).

Ethical and Moral Teaching. Brotherly love is to continue (1:3); they are urged to grow in faith (1:3) and to be obedient to the teaching from the writers (2:15; 3:4). They are to be careful that they are not deceived (2:2,3) and to live calm and untroubled lives (2:2,3). Those who are unruly, or who are busybodies, are to be disciplined in a corrective manner (3:6,14,15).

The Second Coming. The second epistle to the Thessalonians gives special emphasis to the end time. Jesus will be revealed from heaven to give rest to the faithful and to render vengeance on those who do not know God and who have not obeyed the gospel (1:5-10). Some evidently were saying that the Lord had already come, but the readers are assured that He had not, and they are not to allow any such report to disturb them. Before the Lord comes again certain things must take place (2:1-12).

Paul. This epistle tells some things about the apostle's oral teaching while in Thessalonica (2:5). He had taught on a wide variety of subjects as the context shows. 2 Thessalonians is a good source from which we can learn of Paul's deep, personal concern for the converts with whom he had worked. He encourages, warns and urges them to look to the future when, together, they will be in God's very presence.

OUTLINE: 2 Thessalonians

I. Salutation, 1:1,2
II. Encouragement in Persecution, 1:3-12
    A. Thanksgiving, 1:3,4
    B. The Judgment at Christ's Coming 1:5-12
        1. Encouragement in troubles, 1:5-10
        2. Prayer for God's blessings, 1:11,12

III. Explanation of the Day of the Lord, 2:1-17
    A.   The Day not Already Present, 2:1,2
    B.   Events Preceding the Day of the Lord, 2:3-12
        1. First, the rebellion, 2:3
        2. The man of lawlessness to be revealed, 2:4,5
        3. The restrainer taken away, 2:6,7
        4. The man of lawlessness, 2:8-12
    C.   Thanksgiving and Admonition, 2:13-15
    D.   Prayer for the Readers, 2:16,17
IV. Exhortation to the Church, 3:1-18
    A.   Request for Prayers, 3:1,2
    B.   Expression of Confidence in the Lord, 3:3-5
    C.   Working with the Disorderly, 3:6-15
        1. No tolerance for the disorderly, 3:6
        2. Example of the authors, 3:7-9
        3. No work, no food, 3:10
        4. Appeal to the disorderly themselves, 3:11-13
        5. The disorderly to be treated sternly, yet as brothers, 3:14-15
    D.   Conclusion, 3:16-18
        1. Prayer for the readers, 3:16
        2. Sign of authenticity, 3:17,18

Chapter 1

SECOND THESSALONIANS

I. Salutation 1:1,2

V:1 Paul, and Silvanus, and Timothy, unto the church of the Thessalonians in God our Father and the Lord Jesus Christ; V:2 Grace to you and peace from God the Father and the Lord Jesus Christ.

V:1 Paul, and Silvanus, and Timothy, unto the church of the Thessalonians in God our Father and the Lord Jesus Christ;—As in the first epistle Paul, Silvanus and Timothy are mentioned as the authors of the second. It seems certain from the epistle itself that Paul is the real author and the others are joined with him since they were with Paul in Thessalonica. They join with him in the deep concern for the spiritual well-being of the readers. The opening verse is like that of 1 Thessalonians with one addition. Here the word "our" is added to "God our Father." "Our" includes both the writers and the Christians to whom the epistle was written.

V:2 Grace to you and peace from God the Father and the Lord Jesus Christ.—The first words of this verse are in verse 1 of the first epistle, but here the salutation is expanded as is that of 1 and 2 Timothy. "God the Father and the Lord Jesus Christ" is also added after "grace and peace" as is normal in Paul's letters (cf. Romans 1:7; 1 Corinthians 1:3; 2 Corinthians

104

1:2; Galatians 1:3; Ephesians 1:2; Philippians 1:2; Colossians 1:2; Titus 1:4). Notice the repeated emphasis on the deity of Christ indicated in both verses 1 and 2 by the joining "God the Father and the Lord Jesus Christ" as equal.

II. Encouragement in Persecution, 1:3-12

A. Thanksgiving, 1:3,4

V:3 We are bound to give thanks to God always for you, brethren, even as it is meet, for that your faith groweth exceedingly, and the love of each one of you all toward one another aboundeth; V:4 so that we ourselves glory in you in the churches of God for your patience and faith in all your persecutions and in the afflictions which ye endure;

V:3 We are bound to give thanks to God always for you, brethren, even as it is meet,—Again the writers use words very similar to those in 1 Thessalonians 1:2. The major difference here is the use of the words "we are bound" (Greek: *opheilo*) which indicate that the authors had a personal obligation "to give thanks." The suggestions that this verse lacks some of the warmth of its parallel in the first epistle, and is therefore not an authentic work of Paul, is to be rejected. If the readers had protested that they did not deserve such commendation as given in the first epistle, the writers might be expected to reply in this way. Also, it is possible that whoever was in some way opposing the teaching of the missionaries about the coming of Christ at the end time may have claimed that all the words of praise and thanksgiving were just flattery. Either way, the point is clear here that it was "meet" to do so. "Meet" is from a word (Greek: *axion*) which literally means "fitting" or "proper." The words of 1 Thessalonians were not merely words; the recent converts deserved them because of their demonstrated faithfulness even under persecution.

for that your faith groweth exceedingly, and the love of each one of you all toward one another aboundeth;—In 1 Thessalonians 1:3 the writers mention the faith, hope and love of the readers. Two of those graces are mentioned here evidently because the need to grow in these areas is clear from the first epistle. The writers wanted to perfect what was lacking in the faith of the new Christians (1 Thessalonians 3:10) and had prayed that their love might increase and abound (1 Thessalonians 3:12; 4:10). Evidently the response to the first letter had been good and the prayers had been answered. The verb translated "groweth exceedingly" (Greek: *huperauxano*) is found only here in the New Testament. It presents the thought of a very vigorous growth like a tree. The verb "aboundeth" (Greek: *pleonazo*) is the same word used in the prayer in 1 Thessalonians 3:12 and is used here to show that the prayer was answered.

V:4 **so that we ourselves glory in you**—The opening words of this verse indicate that others had reported the progress of the church in Thessalonica and that the progress was so dramatic that those who had laid the foundation of the congregation, who would be expected to remain silent about its growth, could restrain themselves no longer. "Glory" (Greek: *enkauchaomai*) is found only here in the New Testament. The word reminds the reader of a similar statement in 1 Thessalonians 2:19 where the "glorying" (a related form of the word) is at the last day, but here is a present reality. The words "in you" give the ground of the boasting.

in the churches of God—The "churches" are evidently the churches in Achaia. Several times the phrase "churches of God" refers to the Jerusalem church (Galatians 1:13; 1 Corinthians 15:9) or "the Judean churches" (1 Thessalonians 2:14). The point in this place seems to be those churches located where Paul and his co-workers have been.

for your patience and faith—In verse 3, "faith" is general, but here the word is more specifically the faith which enabled the readers to remain patient or steadfast under persecution and other trials (cf. 1 Thessalonians 3:7).

in all your persecutions and in the afflictions which ye endure;—The persecutions and afflictions mentioned here are evidently a continuation of those in 1 Thessalonians 2:14 even though an aorist verb is used there. There is no basis for dating 2 Thessalonians before the first epistle in these verses.

B. The Judgment at Christ's Coming, 1:5-12

1. Encouragement in troubles, 1:5-10

V:5 which is a manifest token of the righteous judgment of God; to the end that ye may be counted worthy of the kingdom of God, for which ye also suffer: **V:6** if so be that it is a righteous thing with God to recompense affliction to them that afflict you, **V:7** and to you that are afflicted rest with us, at the revelation of the Lord Jesus from heaven with the angels of his power in flaming fire, **V:8** rendering vengeance to them that know not God, and to them that obey not the gospel of our Lord Jesus: **V:9** who shall suffer punishment, even eternal destruction from the face of the Lord and from the glory of his might, **V:10** when he shall come to be glorified in his saints, and to be marvelled at in all them that believed (because our testimony unto you was believed) in that day.

V:5 which is a manifest token of the righteous judgment of God;—There are no words for "which is" in the Greek text, but some such insertion is necessary for the English sense. "A manifest token" indicates a proof to the readers that they were able to endure the persecutions and afflictions because God is supplying help and will continue to see them through any future adversities while they keep the faith.

to the end that ye may be counted worthy of the kingdom of God,—These words indicate the intended result of the faithfulness. To "be counted worthy" refers to the fact of their being "fit" for the kingdom, and there is no thought of merit here (cf. Luke 20:35; Acts 5:41). "The kingdom of God" refers to the future manifestation at Christ's coming.

for which ye also suffer:—"For which" (Greek: *huper*) indicates that the suffering is "because of" the kingdom, not in order to inherit the kingdom. Their suffering is brought about because of their citizenship in the kingdom. "Also" seems to be added to show that the readers were enduring the suffering not merely because of their own interest in the kingdom but out of loyalty to the kingdom. The word may simply mean that the readers are suffering in the same way as Paul and his co-workers.

V:6 if so be that it is a righteous thing with God to recompense affliction to them that afflict you, — Mention of the "righteous judgment of God" leads to a vivid description of that judgment. "If so be that" is the translation of one word (Greek: *eiper*) which introduces a conditional clause. There is no doubt about God's righteousness but its reality is assumed. The coming judgment will be righteous because God judges righteously. His verdict will never be arbitrary or capricious but in strict harmony with what is just (cf. Revelation 19:2). "To recompense" means that He will "pay back," and the word implies a full and due requital. Those who "afflict" the Thessalonians, repeatedly subjecting them to various pressures of persecution, will be dealt with in kind by the Judge of all. It is true that God is love and that He is a God of mercy; it is also true that He is a God of justice and of wrath against sin (cf. Romans 11:22; Galatians 6:7).

V:7 and to you that are afflicted rest with us, — God's "paying back" is not limited to the wicked. For the afflicted there is to be a reversal of present experiences. There is a "rest" promised to them. "Rest" is from a word (Greek: *anesis*) which means "a loosing, a relief, a relaxation from strain" and is the opposite of affliction. "With us" refers to Paul, Silvanus and Timothy who knew the problems of persecution, but who had come to realize that something far better awaits the faithful (cf. Romans 8:18-25).

The mention of punishment and rest as "rewards" have caused some to question the ethics of Christian teaching. The following words from Leon Morris are an excellent response to such questions.

> It is true that the Christian must serve his God for what He is, and not from selfish motives. It is true, too, that he who serves in order to obtain a reward has not really caught the spirit of Christianity at all. He has simply exchanged one form of selfishness for another, and the result is not pleasing. Yet when full allowance has been made for that, it remains that the New

Testament does speak of a rest for the people of God (Hebrews 4:9). We are not being true to its teaching if we overlook this. While it may well be true to say that if we are still serving God with a view to something for ourselves we do not know much about the Christian faith, it is also true that the contemplation of the rest that God has reserved for them is a legitimate activity of the saints who are passing through trials (201).

at the revelation of the Lord Jesus—To some extent the wrath of God is being revealed even now (Romans 1:18), but the context here looks to the coming of Christ for judgment. The noun "revelation" is used 13 of 18 times in the New Testament by Paul. The verb form of the word is used by Paul 13 of 26 New Testament occurrences. The basic meaning is the uncovering, or unveiling, what is already in existence so that it can be seen. Jesus Christ certainly exists and will become visible to people again (cf. Revelation 1:7).

from heaven with the angels of his power in flaming fire,— Three prepositional phrases are used to describe the revelation of Jesus Christ. "From heaven" refers to the place from which He will come (cf. 1 Thessalonians 1:10). At present, He sits at "the right hand of the throne of the Majesty in the heavens" (Hebrews 8:1). His return is further described as "with the angels of his power." These are the attendants of the Lord as He comes (cf. Matthew 16:27; 25:31). Since there is no definite article with the word "angels," the expression is qualitative and seems to mean "angels such as are associated with His power." The third phrase, "in flaming fire," points to another accompaniment. These words point to the glory and majesty of the Lord at His coming. The appearance of "the angel of the Lord," or "of the Lord," is often described as being accompanied by fire (Exodus 3:2; 19:18; 24:17; Psalm 18:12; Daniel 7:9,10; cf. Acts 7:30), speaking of the divine majesty and/or indignation against sin. The entire picture emphasizes His glory, might and majesty.

V:8 rendering vengeance to them that know not God,—The future judgment to be carried out by Christ mentioned here is derived at least in part from Daniel 7:13,14. In that passage "the Ancient of Days" gives dominion to the "one like a son of man," who is evidently Jesus Christ. In connection with that, note John 5:27 where the Father gives the Son "authority to execute judgment, because he is a son of man" (cf. Acts 10:42; 17:31). The word translated "vengeance" does not indicate a vindictive spirit of retaliation, but it expresses the thought of administrating justice. "To them that know not God" may, in light of other passages, refer to pagans (Psalm 79:6; Jeremiah 10:25; 1 Thessalonians 4:5). However, some of the Jewish people fit into that same category (Hosea 4:1,6). The ignorance spoken of here is not the inadvertent type, but it is the inexcusable refusal to know God which may be true of any person. The knowledge is not mere intellectual awareness of God's existence, but knowledge which was rejected (Hosea 4:6; Romans 1:18-23). Jesus taught that eternal life consists of knowing God (John 17:3), not knowing Him indicates exclusion from that life. The knowledge which is needed is described as "ethically fruitful knowledge of God" (Bruce, 151).

and to them that obey not the gospel of our Lord Jesus: — The use of the definite article before the words "that obey not the gospel" in the Greek text indicates that two groups of people are meant in this verse: (1) the ones who do not know God, and (2) the ones who do not obey the gospel. The first group are often identified as Gentiles and the second as Jews. Such a distinction may be correct, but it is possible that the structure is the parallelistic style of Old Testament poetry and prophecy. The evidence from grammar favors the thought of two groups but there is no solid evidence to identify the two as Gentiles and Jews respectively.

The word translated "obey" implies a personal and willing response to some message. The message is "the gospel of our Lord Jesus." The ones mentioned here did not so respond.

V:9 who shall suffer punishment, — "Who" refers to all included in verse 8: those who do not know God or who do not obey the gospel. The word "suffer" is not as emphatic as the word for "suffer" in verse 5. This word means simply "undergo" and it is in the future tense, evidently looking to the coming of Christ at the end of the age. "Punishment" (Greek: *dike*) is from the same root word as "righteous" and "vengeance" in the earlier verses. The word generally refers to a penalty imposed by a court of law. The basic meaning has to do with a standard to which something is to conform. It came to express the results of a law suit, "execution of a sentence," thus "punishment." The word considers the punishment from the viewpoint of an unbiased judge.

even eternal destruction from the face of the Lord and from the glory of his might,—There is no word for "even" in the Greek text but it is added to help with the English sense. "Eternal destruction" is a difficult phrase. Grammatically it is an accusative in apposition to "punishment." "Destruction" (Greek: *olethros*) is used in 1 Corinthians 5:5 of the discipline of an erring brother with a view to his spiritual profit; in 1 Timothy 6:9 it is used of the consequences of the indulgence of the flesh; in 1 Thessalonians 5:3 it refers to the calamities which will accompany the return of the Lord at the judgment. The latter meaning is the proper one here. It does not imply annihilation or cessation of being. The word indicates the loss of well-being or ruin in the sense that the person destroyed is unable to fulfill the purpose of his existence. The "punishment" is described by the adjective "eternal." This word expresses the thought of endless, perpetual, or the opposite of "temporal" (cf. 2 Corinthians 4:18). There is no reason to think that this statement means that the punishment is merely final or irreversible. It is final and irreversible but it is more. "Eternal" is the same word used to describe the life promised to the faithful. If it means life without end in that promise why does it not mean that the punishment is endless? The "punishment" or "destruction" being described here is not only without end, it has to do with a quality of existence which is the opposite of the "eternal life" mentioned in Matthew 25:46. There is no punishment if there is no consciousness of it.

The destruction is further described as being "from the face of the Lord and from the glory of his might." That means that it consists of absolute exclusion from the presence of Him in whom is truth, light and life, Jesus Christ (cf. Matthew 25:41; Luke 13:27,28). At least some of the punishment is the awareness of being banished from the Lord's presence with all the joys associated with that presence, and from any participation in the demonstration of His power in glory at the parousia (cf. Colossians 3:4). Remember that there is no punishment if one is not conscious of it and such warnings would have no meaning.

V:10 **when he shall come to be glorified in his saints,**—The wording of this passage indicates a certainty of the coming, but uncertainty as to its time. The coming refers to the "revelation" mentioned in verse 7. There is one single coming at an indefinite future time, not two or more. There are two infinitives used to express purposes of His coming. First, "to be glorified in his saints." The glory of the Lord Jesus Christ will be seen clearly reflected in His people, they being mirrors reflecting that glory. It is possible, but not likely, that the meaning is that Christ will be glorified when the saints are assembled with Him in glorified bodies and perfected in spirit.

and to be marvelled at in all them that believed (because our testimony unto you was believed) in that day.—The second of the infinitive phrases shows that Jesus will come "to be marvelled at." The word "marvelled at" indicates the mingled surprise and admiration evoked in the spectators by this demonstration of love, grace, power and wisdom from God. "In all them that believed" refers to the same group as "saints" in the earlier part of the verse. "In that day" is the occasion of the giving punishment to the wicked and glory to the redeemed, the Day of the Lord so often mentioned in these two epistles. The parenthetic expression shows that the Christians in Thessalonica will be among those who will marvel at the Lord. The preachers proclaimed the gospel and bore witness to the power of that message and the hearers believed it. No doubt, these words are intended to encourage the readers.

2. Prayer for God's blessings, 1:11,12

V:11 To which end we also pray always for you, that our God may count you worthy of your calling, and fulfil every desire of goodness and every work of faith, with power; V:12 that the name of our Lord Jesus may be glorified in you, and ye in him, according to the grace of our God and the Lord Jesus Christ.

Being assured of the true conversion of the Thessalonian Christians and that they have made much progress in their Christian growth, the writers know that they still must live faithful lives daily. In light of that, the writers continue to pray for them.

V:11 To which end we also pray always for you,—The "end" has been stated before in several places: they expected the readers to be a cause for their boasting and rejoicing at the parousia. In this verse the writers assure them of their continuing prayers in their behalf.

that our God may count you worthy of your calling,—The first point in this prayer is that God may act for them. God has called them to holiness in life and to ultimate glory. God alone can "count, consider, or reckon" them as worthy, and He will do so if they continue to conduct themselves in a worthy manner. The "calling" in Thessalonians is twofold: (1) to salvation by believing and obeying the gospel (2 Thessalonians 2:13,14), and (2) it expands the calling to the entrance of the eternal state (1 Thessalonians 1:12; 5:24). The latter is evidently in mind here.

and fulfil every desire of goodness and every work of faith, with power;—The prayer is also that God might "fulfil" or "accomplish" or "make effective" every desire. The word for "every desire" indicates "every good desire" and is used in the New Testament only in reference to those who are acceptable to God. "Of goodness" refers to the desires of the converts, not of God in this context. This part of the prayer shows that man alone is not able to accomplish his good intentions apart from divine help. The prayer also includes the thought that God might fulfil "every work of faith." True faith is demonstrated by works (cf. Ephesians 2:10; James 2:18;

113

1 Thessalonians 1:3). Man does works of faith but God's power is necessary for them to be fulfilled as this prayer shows. This latter point is emphasized by the addition of the words "with power."

V:12 that the name of our Lord Jesus may be glorified in you,—"That" (Greek: *hopos*) introduces a purpose for the prayer in verse 11. "The name of our Lord Jesus" refers to the character and reputation of the Lord. "Name" in the Bible almost always means more than simple identity. Those who continue faithful in their daily living will bring honor to the one they follow. "Be glorified" refers to the present time, in this age, although verse 10 refers to the future day of judgment. "In you" refers to "their daily lives, their conduct, their desires of goodness" and "their works of faith." A genuine Christian life will bring glory to Jesus Christ because it recognizes Him as Lord (Matthew 5:16; 2 Corinthians 9:13; 1 Peter 2:9,12), and an unfaithful life brings reproach upon Him (Hebrews 6:4-6; 10:28,29).

and ye in him,—If the readers live so that Christ is glorified, there will be a reciprocal sharing in the glory. The principle is seen in John 13:31 and the context where Jesus was glorified in His death on the cross and the Father was glorified in Christ's obedience.

according to the grace of our God and the Lord Jesus Christ.—All of the things spoken of in this verse are in accordance with grace. The reciprocal glorification is a reality wherever faithful Christians are found. The use of the definite article before the word "God" and omitting it before "Lord Jesus Christ" does not necessarily mean that this should be translated "our God and Lord, Jesus Christ," or some similar way to indicate only one person. That is a possibility (See N. Turner, *Grammatical Insights into the New Testament*, 16), but in this structure the most likely meaning is that both God the Father and Jesus Christ are individually intended (Bruce, 156,157; Morris, 212). Either way one takes the words, the close relationship between God and Jesus is clear. Both are a source of grace and both must be deity.

Chapter 2

III. Explanation of the Day of the Lord, 2:1-17

A. The Day Not Already Present, 2:1,2

V:1 Now we beseech you, brethren, touching the coming of our Lord Jesus Christ, and our gathering together unto him; V:2 to the end that ye be not quickly shaken from your mind, nor yet be troubled, either by spirit, or by word, or by epistle as from us, as that the day of the Lord is just at hand;

V:1 Now we beseech you, brethren, touching the coming of our Lord Jesus Christ,—A new section begins here but it is not unrelated to what is in chapter one, especially verses 5-10. Both chapters deal with the final judgment, the coming of Christ, and the punishment of the wicked. The major emphasis in chapter one is the coming of Christ, but in this section the concern is more with the coming of the "man of sin."

"Now we beseech you, brethren," introduces the main theme of this chapter. "Beseech" is used to introduce a request or exhortation (cf. 1 Thessalonians 4:1; 5:12). The request is made known in verse 2. The word "touching" is from a preposition (Greek: *huper*) which means in this place "in the interest of," or because of the context "with a view to correcting" the thinking of the people. The concern is their thinking about "the coming of our Lord Jesus Christ," a reference to the end of time. People have always been easily excited about this subject, especially over the time of the event. This epistle is intended to correct any false understanding about the subject.

and our gathering together with him;—The word translated "gathering together" is found only one other time in the New Testament where it refers to a present gathering of Christians for worship (Hebrews 10:25). In this place the word refers to the future gathering of the saints to the Lord at the parousia (cf. Matthew 24:31; Mark 13:27; 1 Thessalonians 4:17). There is no reason to think that these words refer to a different time from that in 1 Thessalonians 4:13-18 as many who hold a dispensationalist view suggest.

V:2 to the end that ye be not quickly shaken from your mind, nor yet be troubled,—The teaching in the first epistle about the coming of the Lord and the believers being taken to be with Him forever was the basis for the hope which encouraged the Thessalonians in their time of persecution. In such a situation, it would have been easy for them to become excited about the imminent return of Christ. It is therefore very appropriate for the writers to address the problem of misunderstanding. "We beseech you,. . .to the end" states the reason for concern about the Christians in Thessalonica. They had been reassured about the future in the first epistle, now they are being reassured about their present experiences; the present afflictions were not evidence that the parousia had occurred. "Be shaken" is from a verb (Greek: *saleuo*) which means "to shake, to cause to move to and fro, to cause to waiver." but in the passive voice, as here, "to be shaken, to be made to waiver or totter." The word can also mean "to agitate or excite" (Luke 6:38; Acts 17:13) and it may be used metaphorically of being so perturbed as to lose one's normal composure and good sense (Marshall, 186). The word "quickly" refers to the ready response to an impression without giving proper consideration to the matter. "From your mind" shows the danger of being separated from your ability to reason. "Mind," in this passage, refers to the entire intellectual concept of man using his powers of judgment. The verb "troubled" is in the present tense and points to a continuing state of agitation following the "shaking" of the previous phrase. The word is used in a similar eschatological context in Matthew 24:6 and Mark 13:7.

either by spirit, or by word, or by epistle as from us, as that the day of the Lord is just at hand;—Three possible methods by which the readers might have been troubled are mentioned. Apparently some attempts had been made by these methods to deceive the Thessalonians as to the Lord's coming. Someone had claimed to receive a message from the Spirit, or by means of the Spirit. Such a message was false if received at all, or it was misunderstood if genuine. "By word" indicates a claim of receiving a message by "spoken word." "Word" is distinguished from "by spirit" and from "by epistle." The claim seems to be that the message was from an apostle or some authority figure to whom attention should be given. However, the claim was false if received. The third claim was based on an epistle which was said to be from Paul and his co-workers. It may be that such a claim is the reason that at the end of this epistle the sign of authenticity of genuine letters is given (3:17). The major point is that no such claim should be allowed to shake the readers or to trouble them.

The report, or reports, mentioned were making the claim "that the day of the Lord is just at hand." "The day of the Lord" was discussed in connection with 1 Thessalonians 5:2. The words translated "as that" (Greek: *hos hoti*) gives a bit of a subjective tone to the clause introduced. The thought is that the day of the Lord is alleged to be "at hand," but the writers completely disassociate themselves from any approval of the claim. There is no word in the Greek text for "just." Apparently the translators added it to bring out their view that the coming was to take place immediately. The phrase "is at hand" is from one Greek word (*enistemi*) which is in the perfect tense. In that tense, the verb means "is now present" in the New Testament. In other places Paul makes a clear distinction between "things present" and "things to come" (Romans 8:38; 1 Corinthians 3:22). The same verb is used in reference to the "present distress that is upon us" (1 Corinthians 7:26) and in reference to "this present evil age" in Galatians 1:4. This meaning for the verb is reflected in most modern translations (cf. ERV, RSV, NEB, NASB, NIV). There is, however, strong support for the view that in this place the word has the sense of imminence rather than actual presence (cf. KJV, ASV). J. B. Lightfoot translates the word "is imminent." He adds, "The Apostle then does not deny that the day of the Lord may be near. He asserts that it is not imminent" (110). It does seem unlikely that the Thessalonians could have been duped into believing that the events described in 1 Thessalonians had already taken place. It is possible that because of the persecution being experienced that they thought the end was beginning. Perhaps their thoughts were like those described in the time of Septimius Severus (shortly after A.D. 200). The persecution of the Christians was so strong that the minds of many were shaken because they thought the appearance of antichrist was at hand (Eusebius, *Ecclesiastical History*, 6.7).

In light of the wording and the context, it seems likely that some were teaching that the second coming had occurred in a silent and invisible way. Whatever may have been in the minds of the people, Paul and his co-workers, who knew more of the situation than anyone today, considered it important enough to give more information about the coming of the day of the Lord. The following verses give that information.

B. Events Preceding the Day of the Lord, 2:3-12

1. First, the rebellion, 2:3

V:3 let no man beguile you in any wise: for it will not be, except the falling away come first, and the man of sin be revealed, the son of perdition,

V:3 let no one beguile you in any wise:—This is a sweeping warning intended to assure the spiritual safety of the readers by alerting them to possible dangers. The structure of the sentence warns against being deceived by anyone no matter who may try to deceive them. "Beguile" is a strong word indicating a thorough deception, whether by wicked intent or simply being misled into a false way of thinking. Church history gives many examples of how often people are quickly attracted by any new fad that comes along. "In any wise" includes the three methods of deception mentioned in verse 2 as well as any other which may be used. Each Christian has the responsibility for himself (Jude 21; John 15:9,10), and the responsiblity to encourage others in right living (Hebrews 3:12-14).

for it will not be, except the falling away come first,—The words "it will not be" are added by the translators to complete the thought for the English reader. The reference is clearly to the day of the Lord. That day will not come until the "falling away" (Greek: *apostasia*), the "apostasy," takes place. The word translated "falling away" refers to a rebellion on the part of professed Christians against God and His truth. The only time element in this statement is that it was future from the time of writing. The translations used in some versions, like "the final rebellion" (NEB; GNB), are based on a view of the future not on the text itself.

and the man of sin be revealed, the son of perdition,—The phrase "man of sin" is a Hebrew idiom used to describe one whose predominate characteristic is sin. The same idiom is in Proverbs 24:5 and Isaiah 53:3 where different characteristics are mentioned. The man here is thought of as completely under the domination of sin so that he is the very embodiment of it. The revealing of "the man of sin" is not something later than the "falling away," but the two are coincident.

There is a variant reading in some of the Greek manuscripts which make the passage refer to "the man of lawlessness" (Greek: *anomos*) instead of "sin" (Greek: *hamartia*). It should be noted that there is little, if any, difference in the statement with either reading. Sin and lawlessness are interchangeable terms since either indicates a disrespect for God and His law (cf. 1 John 3:4). Either term fits with the context of the "falling away."

There has been much discussion as to the identity of "the man of sin." Those who hold that a specific man, or a line of men who hold some office, is intended have suggested many world leaders. Some have suggested Hitler, Stalin, Henry Kissinger or some other well-known person. Many Protestants, especially since the Reformation, have tried to identify "the man of sin" as the Pope or the entire line of Popes. Others since early times have thought the reference was to one of the line of Roman emperors. No one of these suggestions can be shown to fit the Biblical text. Whoever, or whatever, is meant by the phrase was meaningful to the first readers. It is also true that the clear teaching about the coming of Jesus at any time in later New Testament writings, even in 1 Thessalonians 5:2,3, could not be true if the events spoken of here were to take place in the distant future.

Another popular view of "the man of sin" is that he is to be identified as the antichrist of 1 and 2 John and possibly with the beast of Revelation 13:11ff. Some think that he will be some Jewish person, a theory based on Daniel 11:37, but lacking clear evidence from the context. This view is generally held by those of a premillennial dispensational concept of eschatology. This view of things makes it necessary to put the revealing of "the man of sin" just before the return of Christ. There are many problems connected with the theory. Perhaps the first to note is that the text itself does not put the events mentioned in the distant future. The entire theory is based on a certain view of Revelation 20, especially verse 3. There is no Biblical reason to identify "the man of sin" with antichrist or the beast nor to place these events in the distant future from the time of writing.

No one is able to identify "the man of sin" with absolute certainty. It seems best to see the words as personifying the basic principle of evil at work in the world seeking to lead people away from God and truth into sin. The system was already at work when the words were written as 2:7 clearly says.

"The son of perdition" (Greek: *apoleia*) is a phrase used to describe "the man of sin." Since this one, whoever or whatever he is, is characterized by his opposition to God, he is doomed to destruction, that is, ruin or loss of well-being. The same words are used to describe Judas in John 17:12.

2. The man of sin to be revealed, 2:4,5

V:4 he that opposeth and exalteth himself against all that is called God or that is worshipped; so that he sitteth in the temple of God, setting himself forth as God. V:5 Remember ye not, that, when I was yet with you, I told you these things?

V:4 he that opposeth and exalteth himself against all that is called God or that is worshipped;—The man of sin is further described in this verse. "He that opposeth" is the translation of a participle with a definite article. The basic verb (Greek: *antikeimai*) means "to set over against," "adversary," or simply "to oppose." It is used of those who opposed Jesus (Luke 13:17); of those who opposed His people (Luke 21:15; 1 Corinthians 16:9; Philippians 1:28); or those who opposed His teaching (1 Timothy 1:10). The same verb is used to express the mutual antagonism between the spirit and the flesh in the Christians (Galatians 5:17). In the Greek version of the Old Testament it is used of Satan (Zechariah 3:1) as well as in the New Testament (1 Timothy 5:14). It seems clear, however, that Satan is not meant in this verse. The one called "the man of sin" also "exalteth himself against (literally "over") all that is called God or that is worshipped." The participle "exalteth himself" is in the middle voice which gives it a reflexive force. This one quite literally exalts himself highly against the very concept of Deity. He also exalts himself against every object of reverence whether pagan, Jewish or Christian.

so that he sitteth himself in the temple of God, setting himself forth as God.—"So that" (Greek: *hoste*) followed by an infinitive usually indicates result. The thought here is that "he opposes. . .and so exalts himself as that he sits." "Sitteth" is an aorist active infinitive from *kathizo* and indicates the taking of the seat instead of a continuing in the seat. The preposition translated "in" (Greek: *eis*) used with the accusative case implies motion toward and shows that the man of sin puts himself "into" God's seat in the temple. "The temple of God" has been identified with the church, the inner sanctuary of the Jerusalem temple which was destroyed in A.D. 70, a temple which many think will be built in the future, and the suggestion that the reference is metaphorical and/or typological based on statements in Ezekiel or Daniel, but using that to portray the final manifestation of evil as an anti-theistic power which usurps the place of God in the world. In the latter suggestion there would be no specific temple, but the language refers to the claim to be God which expresses the opposition of evil to God. The last view seems to be the best of these. The principle of evil may well take different forms at different times depending on circumstances.

"Setting himself forth as God" is a strong statement. The literal meaning is something like "proclaiming himself to be God," or "announcing that I myself am God." The claim is not that he is the God of Jesus and Christians, but that he is God, the absolute and exclusive God.

V:5 Remember ye not, that, when I was yet with you, I told you these things?—The use of the first person singular shows that Paul was evidently the actual author of this epistle (cf. 1 Thessalonians 5:27). While Paul and his co-workers were in Thessalonica instruction about the man of sin and the subsequent claims were given. The readers are called upon to remember the details which had been presented earlier. Those first readers no doubt knew exactly what these verses meant. Note that the word "told" is the translation of a word that indicates a repetition of the teaching. The wording of the question shows that a "yes" was expected in their response.

3. The restrainer taken away, 2:6,7

V:6 And now ye know that which restraineth, to the end that he may be revealed in his own season. V:7 For the mystery of lawlessness doth already work: only there is one that restraineth now, until he be taken out of the way.

V:6 And now ye know that which restraineth,—There is some disagreement as to the exact function of the adverb "now." It is best to take it as in the ASV where it is related to "ye know." The force of the word is evidently resumptive and continues the sense of verse 5: "You remember what I told you while I was there, and now you know for yourselves." They knew because they had been told. "That which restraineth" is a present active participle neuter accusative singular form. The restraining force has been identified as the Jewish state, the Roman state, Paul himself and even James of Jerusalem. Others have suggested that the restrainer is the Holy Spirit, the preaching of the gospel or God at work in the universe. More than one of these could be intended by the neuter verbal form here but the use of the masculine form in verse 7 in reference to the same thing raises some problems. The Christians in Thessalonica knew because Paul had told them. We, however, have not been told and any identification is a guess. My suggestion (guess) is that it is a reference to God at work in the universe. That harmonizes with the use of the neuter and the masculine in the respective statements. It also is in harmony with other Scripture.

to the end that he may be revealed in his own season.—The structure here, a preposition plus the definite article plus an infinitive, could mean "until he is revealed at his proper time," but it is more likely that the meaning is as in the text used: "to the end..." The purpose is God's purpose and it is clear that both the man of sin and the restrainer are under His ultimate control. "In his own season" indicates that there is a "proper time" in God's scheme for this revelation.

V:7 For the mystery of lawlessness doth already work:—The word "mystery" (Greek: *musterion*) is used in the New Testament in reference to what has been concealed from man but now is revealed by God in the disclosure of His purpose. "The mystery of lawlessness" is apparently to be understood of a satanic counterpart to the mystery of God's purpose. At the time of writing, it was already at work, but largely hidden under the surface. Enough was known about it to know that it was already working at the time.

only there is one that restraineth now, until he be taken out of the way.—The restrainer is here considered as personal and of limited duration. The structure is awkward and somewhat difficult to put into good English (Compare the versions), but the sense is clear in the ASV. Evil was at work, but not fully revealed. It was under restraint at the time of writing, but the restraint was to be removed in due time.

There has been much discussion about the identity of the restrainer, but no one can be certain about the matter. We can know that God is in control and His purpose will be accomplished.

4. The man of lawlessness, 2:8-12

V:8 And then shall be revealed the lawless one, whom the Lord Jesus shall slay with the breath of his mouth, and bring to nought by the manifestation of his coming; V:9 even he, whose coming is according to the working of Satan with all power and signs and lying wonders, V:10 and with all deceit of unrighteousness for them that perish; because they received not the love of the truth, that they might be saved. V:11 And for this cause God sendeth them a working of error, that they should believe a lie: V:12 that they all might be judged who believed not the truth, but had pleasure in unrighteousness.

V:8 And then shall be revealed the lawless one,—"And then" is used in contrast to the "and now" in verse 6. "Shall be revealed" marks the third time this word has been used of the lawless one (verses 3,6,8). At the proper time the lawless one will be revealed but only after the events of verse 7 take place. This clause, introduced by "and then," closes the argument in verse 6 and 7 and opens the door for two very important points: (1) "whom the Lord will slay," and (2) the significance of the "coming" of the lawless one.

whom the Lord Jesus shall slay with the breath of his mouth,—The word "slay" (Greek: *anaireo*) may mean "to take away, destroy, kill." The word is used of murder and in this verse it suggests that the end of the lawless one will be as decisive as that of one who is murdered. The reading "shall consume" in the KJV is based on a text with less support. That reading (Greek: *analisko*) suggests destruction by fire. The reading of the ASV is preferred. "With the breath of his mouth" reflects the thought of Isaiah 11:4 and names the instrument of destruction which Jesus will employ. The word "breath" is from *pneuma*, "spirit, wind, breath," and may indicate His word or His breath itself. The former seems most likely.

and bring to nought by the manifestation of his coming; — The verb translated "bring to nought" is *katargeo*. It is a word with several possible translations as demonstrated in the various English versions. See Leon Morris (230) for more on the difficulties of how to translate this word. In this verse the idea is that the lawless one will be rendered idle or inoperative. He will not be seen as significant any longer. The word defines to some extent what the slaying will involve. "By the manifestation of his coming" is a parallel statement of means. "Manifestation" (Greek: *epiphaneia*) is used elsewhere in the New Testament only in Timothy and Titus. Once (2 Timothy 1:10) of the first coming in the flesh, all the other uses refers to the second coming of Christ as it does here. "Coming" (Greek: *parousia*) is the common term for the second coming of Christ. The combination of the two words emphasizes that the entire system involved in the lawless one will be put out of operation by the very radiance of the Lord's presence.

V:9 even he, whose coming is according to the working of Satan with all power and signs and lying wonders, —Translators have properly added the words "even he" to show that the following words refer to the lawless one. By using the word "coming" (Greek: *parousia*), Paul seems to set his coming in deliberate contrast to that of Christ. His "coming is according to the working of Satan." The verb "is" is a present tense and shows the certainty of his coming. He "working," a word used generally in reference to God's power, has its source in Satan; that is, his working will be in harmony and agreement with the character of Satan. He is not Satan, but is inspired by him. "Signs and wonders" are both used to describe the miracles of Christ and His apostles (Acts 2:22,43; 4:30; Romans 15:9; Hebrews 2:4), but here refer to the work of the lawless one. "Signs" point to something observable and indicate some significance lying behind the act or acts, "wonders" refers to something exceptional that causes one to wonder or marvel.

125

The word "lying" evidently describes all three of the nouns: power, signs and wonders. The sense is that the lawless one will be working with a display of all kinds of power demonstrated with signs and wonders calculated to deceive.

V:10 and with all deceit of unrighteousness for them that perish;—More is made known about the working of the lawless one. Having mentioned that he will come with all kinds of power, it is now made known that his work will include all kinds of deception that wickedness can devise. Like his master, he is a deceiver and he uses that ability continually. He intends to deceive "them that perish," or more literally, "them that are perishing," that is, the ones who are already perishing. He wants to keep them in that condition and, if possible, get them into even greater sins. Just what form his deceptive acts take is not revealed. Of course, Satan and his agents are trying to deceive Christians as well, but in this verse the unbeliever is mentioned.

because they received not the love of the truth, that they might be saved.—The conjunction introducing this clause is found only here in Paul's writings. It is used by Luke (Luke 1:20; 19:44; Acts 12:23) in contexts of judgment on wrongdoing. "They received not the love of the truth" shows clearly that the ones mentioned are responsible for their own lostness. "Received" is from *dechomai* and implies ample opportunity but an attitude that did not welcome, or receive with gladness, the truth presented. The "truth" is the gospel message. One who does not receive the truth lays himself open to all types of error (cf. Romans 1:18-28). The last clause, "that they might be saved," goes closely with the former clause: To receive the love of the truth leads to salvation; to refuse the truth leads to destruction.

V:11 And for this cause God sendeth them a working of error, that they should believe a lie:—Because they do not love the truth (cf. John 3:19), God sends a working of error. "Sendeth" is a present tense indicating a constant principle because the mystery of lawlessness was already at work and God's wrath was already in force (cf. Romans 1:18; 2 Corinthians 4:4). Those who refuse to accept truth find that judgment comes upon them in the form of an inability to accept it. The contrast is seen in 1 Thessalonians 2:13. "Working of error" is literally "a power of delusion" sent by God with the intended result that they believe the lie of verse 4. Of course, God has always allowed men to choose their own way, but they also must suffer the consequences. Isaiah taught that principle some 700 years before Paul (Isaiah 66:3,4). The same principle is in Romans 1:24,26,28 where it is stated that "God gave them up" because they refused to follow truth and did what they wanted to do. It may well be said that the means by which one is deceived is God's permissive agency — not God's direct agency (Kelcy, 157). Satan is always limited by God. God allows the temptations whether of deception, suffering, rebellions or whatever causes people to reject the truth. "A lie" is literally "the lie" and evidently refers to the basic denial of the basic truth that God is God which results in worship directed to someone or something else such as "the man of sin." It is first man's choice of what to believe, then the moral and spiritual law of God is carried out.

V:12 that they all might be judged who believe not the truth,—These words tell the purpose of God's action mentioned in verse 11. "Judged" is an aorist passive subjunctive form of *krino* which indicates a once for all action of condemnation. Morris (235) correctly points out that the use of this word instead of one that signifies condemnation and nothing more stresses the judicial purpose of God. God's action is just.

but had pleasure in unrighteousness.—To reject truth is not merely an academic exercise, it affects one's entire life. "Truth" and "falsehood" have moral implications because to reject truth means that one rejects God and His word. That type person will delight in unrighteousness and will be judged as an active doer of that which is the opposite of truth. Note the similar point in Romans 2:8 and its opposite in 1 Corinthians 13:6.

C. Thanksgiving and Admonition, 2:13-15

V:13 But we are bound to give thanks to God always for you, brethren beloved of the Lord, for that God chose you from the beginning unto salvation in sanctification of the Spirit and belief of the truth: V:14 whereunto he called you through our gospel, to the obtaining of the glory of our Lord Jesus Christ. V:15 So then, brethren, stand fast, and hold the traditions which ye were taught, whether by word, or by epistle of ours.

V:13 But we are bound to give thanks to God always for you, brethren beloved of the Lord,— Having answered the speculations about the man of sin, Paul turns to a subject introduced in 1 Thessalonians 1:4. The language is very much like that of 2 Thessalonians 1:3 and emphasizes that he and his co-workers were "bound" to thank God for the readers. This statement is stronger than that in 1:3 since it is reinforced by the use of the word "we" in an emphatic position. The repetition of "always" implies that he saw the readers as consistent in their living, so the thanksgiving should be consistent. "Beloved" is a perfect participle which emphasizes that the readers had been loved by God from a point of time in the past and were still objects of His love at the time of writing.

for that God chose you from the beginning unto salvation in sanctification of the Spirit and belief of the truth: — Paul gives an explanation for the expression in the first part of the verse which is introduced by *hoti*, "for that," as in 1 Thessalonians 2:13 and 1:3 of this second epistle. The reason for this summary of events was to encourage the faint-hearted. Not only have they been chosen, they were in God's scheme from the beginning (cf. 1 Corinthians 2:7; Ephesians 1:4; 3:5,6,11). God had purposed from the beginning to call Gentiles as well as Jews into His eternal Kingdom. The words do not mean that God chose specific individuals for salvation unconditionally. The gospel was to be proclaimed and any person would be chosen only when he heard and responded in faith to the message (cf. verse 14). The fact that the object of "chose" is "you" does not change the meaning of the passage.

God's purpose was to save and the means by which it was to be accomplished was "in sanctification of the Spirit." "Sanctification" (Greek: *hagiasmos*) basically means to be set apart for God (cf. 1 Thessalonians 4:3) and that was, and is, accomplished by the Holy Spirit as one follows His teaching. The process will be completed at the second coming (1:10). The Spirit's work is clearly connected with "belief of the truth." The contrast between the ones spoken of here and those "who believed not the truth, but had pleasure in unrighteousness" is very clear. The "truth" is God's revelation of how men may be made righteous through Jesus Christ, that is, the gospel.

V:14 whereunto he called you through our gospel.—"Whereunto" refers to the salvation into which God called people. "Called" is the aorist tense and points to the time when the gospel was heard and responded to in obedience. The call was actually the gospel being preached, and the reception of it made the call effectual in one's life. God still calls people in the same way today. "Our gospel" is the gospel accepted and preached by the writers of 1 and 2 Thessalonians.

to the obtaining of the glory of our Lord Jesus Christ.—The call from God has a clear purpose in view: the obtaining of the glory of Christ. This glory is shared in this life to some extent (1 Thessalonians 2:12; 2 Thessalonians 1:12), but the emphasis here is on the glory to be shared at the parousia (1:10; cf. 1 John 3:2). Note that the word "obtaining" does not mean that man by his own efforts can earn salvation. New Testament teaching is clear that salvation is from God through Jesus Christ, but that it is experienced only by those who respond in faithful obedience.

V:15 So then, brethren, stand fast,—"So then" links the following closely to the preceding verse and shows that the purpose of that statement was to provide a foundation for the command which now follows. "Stand fast" is repeated from 1 Thessalonians 3:8, or at least the emphasis is from there. This need is one of the central points in these epistles. Here the point is specifically to the danger of being led astray by false teaching.

and hold the traditions which ye were taught,—One way to stand firm is to keep holding to what had been handed down, "the traditions," from Paul and his co-workers. Had there been a firm grasp on basic Christian doctrine and a consistent stability in practice, there would have been no need for this epistle.

whether by word, or by epistle of ours.—The "traditions" to be held were primarily delivered by word of mouth. Paul had told the readers about these matters during the time spent among them (cf. 1 Thessalonians 1:5,6; 2:13; 2 Thessalonians 2:5). Paul also mentions a written document in this verse. The reference is no doubt to the first epistle. No distinction is made between the authority of the spoken and written word. The words which are very important in the statement are "of ours." This phrase calls to mind the teaching, whether by word or epistle, which had caused some confusion about the time of the second coming in 2:2,3. Only those communications from Paul and his co-workers were to be accepted (Note 3:17). It is important to remember that Paul urges his readers to hold to what he and his fellow-preachers handed down, not what might develop later.

D. Prayer for the Readers, 2:16,17

V:16 Now our Lord Jesus Christ himself, and God our Father who loved us and gave us eternal comfort and good hope through grace, V:17 comfort your hearts and establish them in every good work and word.

V:16 Now our Lord Jesus Christ himself, and God our Father who loved us and gave us eternal comfort and good hope through grace,—The prayer beginning in verse 16 is very similar in language to the one in 1 Thessalonians 3:11-13. The writer knew that the Christians in Thessalonica could not accomplish all that was needed in their own strength. In this short prayer he turns their attention to the source of the help needed. The placement of Jesus before the Father is not unusual since Paul does the same in 2 Corinthians 13:14 and in Galatians 1:1. Even though there is a plural subject, the two attributive participles, "who loved us and gave us," are singular as are the two verbs, "comfort" and "establish," in verse 17. The point is that both the Father and the Son are the source of help. The source of "eternal comfort" and "good hope" is also found in both (John 3:16; Galatians 1:4). Note that both "comfort" and "hope" are "through grace."

V:17 comfort your hearts, — Comfort means more than a pat on the back accompanied by soothing words. The word means basically "to give strength, to encourage" so that one is able to cope with the trials that lie ahead. The verb is in the aorist optative form and is best taken as a wish-prayer.

and establish them in every good work and word. — "Establish" also has the thought of strengthening so that one is stable and firm. The Christian should be so intune with God and His Word that his entire life — work and word — is lived in the confidence of God's love and purpose so that he rejects temptations regardless of immediate consequences.

Chapter 3

IV. Exhortation to the Church, 3:1-18

A. Request for prayers, 3:1,2

V:1 Finally, brethren, pray for us, that the word of the Lord may run and be glorified, even as also it is with you; V:2 and that we may be delivered from unreasonable and evil men; for all have not faith.

V:1 Finally, brethren, pray for us,—Although "finally" may point to the conclusion of a letter as in 2 Corinthians 13:11 or Ephesians 6:10, it does not necessarily do so (cf. Philippians 3:1; 4:8 and 1 Thessalonians 4:1). The word may point to additional important exhortations of a more practical nature (cf. 1 Thessalonians 4:1-5:22). "Pray for us" is a request made by Paul to his friends in several churches (Romans 15:30; 2 Corinthians 1:11; Ephesians 6:18-20; Philippians 1:19; Colossians 4:3,4). Here the wording is almost identical with that in the first epistle (5:25) but is more specific. The verb is in the present tense and means "keep on praying."

that the word of the Lord may run and be glorified, even as also it is with you;—Prayers for Paul and his fellow preachers were to be specifically that the "word of the Lord," the gospel, might spread swiftly and that it would "be glorified." which apparently means that it be victorious in the lives of the hearers. God's word is not dead and void of life, but it is living and active (Hebrews 4:12). If the "word of the Lord" runs it will be because Christians are actively proclaiming that word in the world. It is only by the word being made known that men and women can come to faith and thus the word be glorified (cf. Romans 10:17).

The added comment, "even as also it is with you," is evidently a reference to the reception of the gospel among the Thessalonian people (1 Thessalonians 1:2-10). The words "it is" are added by the translators with the intention of making the statement clear. However, the addition limits the words unnecessarily. Paul's words seem more naturally to include the early reception of the gospel while he and his co-workers were still in Thessalonica as well as the continued reception of that word even while writing this epistle.

V:2 and that we may be delivered from unreasonable and evil men;—The second clause of the petition is that Paul and the other missionaries be delivered from their enemies (cf. Romans 15:31). The word "delivered" (Greek: *rhuomai*) means literally "to draw to oneself" but came to mean "rescue or deliver" (G. Abbott-Smith). The obstacles which prevented the swift spread and glorification of the "word of the Lord" where Paul was working, and in Thessalonica, was in human opposition. "Unreasonable" (Greek: *atopos*) basically means "out of place, not fitting, odd, unbecoming, outrageous, improper" (Moulton-Milligan). The writer has in mind those who were capable of outrageous conduct. This word has to do with behavior while the next refers to character. "And evil men" refers to a particular class of men as the use of the definite article makes clear (in the Greek text). These were people who were actively attempting to corrupt others, and may well be a reference to the Jewish antagonists mentioned in Acts 18:12ff. and in 1 Thessalonians 2:16.

for all have not faith.—The word "faith" evidently refers to the Christian faith. Admittedly the word could mean "faithfulness" or "fidelity," but has those meanings elsewhere only in reference to God. Some suggest "trust" as the meaning here, but that is very doubtful. The concept is that not all believe in Jesus Christ as Lord and Savior, or that not all hold to the body of Christian teaching (cf. Jude 3). One thing is clear, the opponents were not in the church but were unbelievers.

B. Expression of Confidence in the Lord, 3:3-5

V:3 But the Lord is faithful, who shall establish you, and guard you from the evil one. V:4 And we have confidence in the Lord touching you, that ye both do and will do the things which we command. V:5 And the Lord direct your hearts into the love of God, and into the patience of Christ.

V:3 But the Lord is faithful,—The play on words—"faith" and "faithful" here—is not an unusual thing in Paul. No doubt he intended to make a contrast between the Lord and the ones who do not have faith. Those who put their faith in the Lord can count on Him being faithful to all His word. "Lord" evidently refers to Jesus Christ here although Paul may not have had a conscious distinction between the Father and Son in mind.

who shall establish you,—These words call to mind the prayers of 1 Thessalonians 3:13 and 2 Thessalonians 2:17. The apostle turns from his own situation to that of the readers. The Lord would not leave them helpless, but would provide a way of escape from every temptation (1 Corinthians 10:13).

and guard you from the evil one.—This is reminiscent of the words in the last part of Matthew 6:13. "The evil" is most likely to be taken as a reference to the personal devil rather than to evil in general in order to form a contrast between the personal Lord and the devil. "The faith" that they hold will be the basis for the help needed.

V:4 And we have confidence in the Lord touching you,—The thought of confidence continues: confidence in the Lord was expressed, now confidence in the readers is expressed because they were in the Lord. Paul is paving the way to the commands given in verses 6-15 which he intends the readers to accept and follow.

that ye both do and will do the things which we command.—There is no doubt about the loyalty of the readers and none is anticipated in the future. The obedience in the past was the basis for confidence that they would obey in the future and that future confidence is where the emphasis is placed here (cf. Findley, 202). The word "command" (Greek: *parangello*) indicates an order that has authority behind it.

V:5 And the Lord direct your hearts into the love of God,— Even though the apostle has complimented the converts, there is no indication that they were self-sufficient. Because of that, he prays that the Lord will direct, or make straight, or remove obstacles, their hearts so that they will concentrate their entire life to the love of God. The phrase "the love of God" may mean either (1) God's love for us, or (2) our love for God. In Paul's writing the former is the normal usage of the phrase. It may be permissible to take this phrase as comprehensive and include both meanings in this place with a slight emphasis on the first (cf. Lightfoot, 127, 128).

and into the patience of Christ.—The same type problem is here as in the previous phrase. It is generally agreed, however, that these words refer to the patience, or steadfastness, of Christ demonstrated in His endurance (Hebrews 12:1-3).

Without being too dogmatic, the two phrases may be paraphrased: "May the Lord teach and enable you to love as God loves, and to be patient as Christ is."

C. Working with the Disorderly, 3:6-15

1. Do not tolerate disorderly conduct, 3:6

V:6 Now we command you, brethren, in the name of our Lord Jesus Christ, that ye withdraw yourselves from every brother that walketh disorderly, and not after the tradition which they received of us.

V:6 Now we command you, brethren, in the name of our Lord Jesus Christ,—In verse 4 the writers mentioned their confidence in the readers to do "the things which we command." In this verse, at least one of those commands is set out explicitly. The topic of disorderly conduct is introduced in 1 Thessalonians 4:11,12 and 5:14. Some of the Thessalonians had not followed the advice given in the first epistle, so Paul commands, or charges (Greek: *parangello*), them in the name of Christ. That charge indicates authority as well as an appeal to do the thing as His servants and to His honor and glory.

that ye withdraw yourselves from every brother that walketh disorderly, and not after the tradition which they received of us.—Some were walking in a disorderly manner, that is, they had failed to follow the instructions given in the first epistle: to be quiet, to do their own business, to work with their hands, to walk properly before nonbelievers, and some were described as "disorderly" even then (1 Thessalonians 4:11,12; 5:14). From such the faithful were to "withdraw themselves," that is, to "keep aloof from" them. The word "disorderly" (Greek: *ataktos*) basically means "disorderly, irregularly; out of step; lazily," but the nature of the matter can be inferred only from the context, especially the following verses. Those from whom the readers should withdraw do not live in harmony with the traditions from Paul and his co-workers. These traditions, teachings, had been given orally (verse 10) and in writing in the first epistle. The teaching relates to personal, daily conduct. The conduct to be marked was that which was out of harmony with Christian principles. It seems certain that idleness was one of the matters involved in the context. The statement "which they received" shows that it was the very ones who had received Paul's instructions who were disobeying them. The purpose of such actions was to keep the congregation pure and to preserve the distinctive Christian identity. Compare a similar admonition in Romans 16:17,18.

2. Example of the authors, 3:7-9

V:7 For yourselves know how ye ought to imitate us: for we behaved not ourselves disorderly among you; V:8 neither did we eat bread for nought at any man's hand, but in labor and travail, working night and day, that we might not burden any of you: V:9 not because we have not the right, but to make ourselves an ensample unto you, that ye should imitate us.

V:7 For yourselves know how ye ought to imitate us:—The writers of the epistle appeal once again to the knowledge of the readers. Such an appeal has already been made a number of times before, in the first epistle 10 times and in the second in 2:6. The word "imitate" means "to mimic" and is used by Paul several times. The sense here is that the readers should follow the pattern of words as well as the example of the missionaries. Specifically here, the reference is to being busy instead of idle. Note that the word "ought" (Greek: *dei*) gives authority to these words and shows that, if they want to be acceptable to the Lord, it is necessary for them to imitate the preachers.

for we behaved not ourselves disorderly among you;—Those men who first carried the gospel to Thessalonica did not do anything out of line nor were they idle. Mention was made about their behavior among the people in 1 Thessalonians 2:9-12, and the following verses in this context emphasize the point again.

V:8 neither did we eat bread for nought at any man's hand,—Paul and his companions did not take support while in Thessalonica in order to be a good example. It would not have been wrong for them to be supported as Jesus Himself had made clear (Matthew 10:10), but they were concerned that they not be a stumbling block to anyone.

but in labor and travail, working night and day, that we might not burden any of you:—"But" is a strong adversative conjunction (Greek: *alla*) and shows that the missionaries' action was the opposite of those being warned against. Paul and the others worked hard and constantly, "night and day," to accomplish their purpose (cf. 1 Thessalonians 2:9; 2 Corinthians 11:9). The preachers did not want to be a burden financially or otherwise to the new converts.

V:9 not because we have not the right, but to make ourselves an ensample unto you, that ye should imitate us.—In addition to Jesus' teaching that "the laborer is worthy of his food" (Matthew 10:10), Paul later expressed the same point in 1 Corinthians 9:4,5, but he adds that he passed up his right because he did not want to give any reason for anyone to find grounds for charging him with any selfish motive. They refused to be a burden "in order that they might present themselves as examples." The word "ensample" is an old word for "example" or "pattern" (see 1 Thessalonians 1:7). The last clause is a purpose clause showing that the writers wanted to undermine the claims of those who were disorderly. If those who had a right to be supported gave up their right, how much more should those who have no right to support be willing to work.

3. No work, no food, 3:10

V:10 For even when we were with you, this we commanded you, If any will not work, neither let him eat.

V:10 For even when we were with you, this we commanded you, If any will not work, neither let him eat.— Paul turns from the example set before the readers to instructions which had been repeatedly given in person. The stress in the verse is on the instruction, or the tradition, given. Since the people of Thessalonica were basically Greek in culture, they believed that work was for slaves. Teaching about the need to work was given consistently from Paul's time in Thessalonica onward as is reflected in the *Didache* 12:3,4: Speaking of one who "comes in the Name of the Lord," he is to be received and helped, but if he "settles among you and has a craft, let him work for his bread. But if he has no craft provide for him according to your understanding, so that no man shall live among you in idleness because he is a Christian" (Dated about A.D. 130).

Paul's command is clear: "If any will not work, neither let him eat." It is an imperative and is concerned with an unwillingness to work, not with an inability. Similar statements are found in both Jewish and Greek writings, but no exact parallel has been found. It seems most likely that this is a Christian ethical principle first stated by Paul.

4. Appeal to the disorderly themselves, 3:11-13

V:11 For we hear of some that walk among you disorderly, that work not at all, but are busybodies. V:12 Now them that are such we command and exhort in the Lord Jesus Christ, that with quietness they work, and eat their own bread. V:13 But ye, brethren, be not weary in well-doing.

V:11 For we hear of some that walk among you disorderly, that work not at all, but are busybodies.—Perhaps this information came together with the information that brought about the misunderstanding about the coming of Christ. It may be that the news had come more than once since he used the present tense verb to express it. The news was about the disorderly conduct on the part of some among them. They were idle which contributed to the movement toward being "busybodies." "Busybodies" comes from a verb which means "to work around, to waste one's energy" and then "to be a busybody." Those were not taking care of their own business but were very busy in other people's business (1 Thessalonians 4:11; 1 Peter 4:15).

V:12 Now them that are such we command and exhort in the Lord Jesus Christ,—The use of both verbs adds emphasis to the statement. The injunction given "in the Lord Jesus Christ" conveys the authority of the Lord behind the words and implies that since both the writers and readers are "in Christ" as members of His body, there should be no more delay in correcting the situation.

that with quietness they work, and eat their own bread.— "With quietness" points to a disposition of mind not found among the readers earlier. They already looked at work with disdain and with the excitement about the Lord's coming, they were rejecting the clear need to work, a matter about which they had been warned. They needed to earn their own living and no longer be in need of support from others. Neil adequately sums up the matter: "Stop fussing, stop idling, and stop sponging" (195).

V:13 But ye, brethren, be not weary in well-doing.—"But ye" presents a contrast between the ones described as "disorderly" and those who are not in that group. The structure of the sentence indicates that Paul is urging them never to become weary in well-doing. "Weary" is from a word that may mean "to behave badly, to be cowardly, to lose courage or to faint." "Well-doing" means doing good or doing noble things. Here it is used as the opposite of "disorderly."

5. The disorderly to be treated sternly, yet as brothers, 3:14,15

V:14 And if any man obeyeth not our word by this epistle, note that man, that ye have no company with him, to the end that he may be ashamed. V:15 And yet count him not as an enemy, but admonish him as a brother.

V:14 And if any man obeyeth not our word by this epistle,— The verb translated "obeyeth" is in the present tense which would be the proper word from the readers viewpoint. "This epistle" refers to the one being read not one that the Thessalonians are expected to write. The Christians in Thessalonica were to take action against those who do not "hold the traditions" (2:15) or who "walketh disorderly" (3:6). Obedience to what the apostle taught is a test of discipleship because it is in fact the word of God (cf. 1 Thessalonians 2:13).

note that man,—"Note" (Greek: *semeioo*) means more than to notice one. It means "to mark, to mark out, to take note of," and indicates a serious matter. The use of the middle voice seems to indicate "to take note for yourself" and makes it a personal responsibility. Careful distinction was to be made between those who obey and those who do not. This word is found only here in the New Testament. For a similar point see Romans 16:17.

that ye have no company with him,— Such disobedient folk should not be included in any social activities which might encourage them or lead them into thinking that their actions were being approved. The thought is similar to that in 1 Corinthians 5:9-11, but the words here suggest a less severe treatment than those.

to the end that he be ashamed.—The command to "have no company with him" is designed to bring the disobedient person back to his rightful position in the congregation and with the Lord. "That he may be ashamed" emphasizes that he needs to repent and that fact needs to be impressed upon him, thus the passive voice of the verb "to be turned in (upon oneself)" (Findlay).

V:15 And yet count him not as an enemy, but admonish him as a brother.—These words bring to mind the fact that problems in the church bring personal feelings into the matter of discipline. The disobedient one is a brother in Christ even though he is for the moment a disobedient one. He needs to be admonished (Greek: *noutheteo*) which literally means "to correct" or "to warn" as a brother, not an enemy (cf. Galatians 6:1). The purpose, as always in such contexts, is to bring him to repentance. Note the use of this word in Acts 20:31; Romans 15:14; 1 Corinthians 4:14; Colossians 1:28; 3:16; 1 Thessalonians 5:12,14.

D. Conclusion, 3:16-18

1. Prayer for the readers, 3:16

V:16 Now the Lord of peace himself give you peace at all times in all ways. The Lord be with you all.

V:16 Now the Lord of peace himself give you peace at all times in all ways.—"Now" (Greek: *de*) again marks the transition from command and exhortation to prayer. "The Lord of peace" indicates something of His character and emphasizes that He alone can bring genuine peace. The phrase "at all times" does not indicate a peace that comes in a series of events, but it indicates a continuous state of peace. "In all ways" asks that the peace continue no matter what the outward circumstance may be. The verb "give" is in the optative mood and expresses a prayerful expectation or wish: "Now may the Lord of peace himself give" (Moule, 136).

The Lord be with you all.—The prayer is essentially repeated and summed up in these words. The Lord had promised to be with His people (Matthew 28:20) and that He would not fail nor forsake them (Hebrews 13:5), but those promises are conditional. They are certain only so long as the ones promised are faithful. If anyone, or all of them, is consistently unfaithful, the Lord will forsake him (cf. Romans 1:24,26,28).

2. Sign of authenticity, 3:17,18

V:17 The salutation of me Paul with mine own hand, which is the token in every epistle: so I write. V:18 The grace of our Lord Jesus Christ be with you all.

V:17 The salutation of me Paul with mine own hand,—It seems that Paul generally dictated his epistles and then wrote the last few sentences in his own hand. That seems to have been the custom of most writers in the same time period. Such a practice would accomplish two things: (1) it showed authenticity, and (2) it made the letter more personal. The special mention of his own hand here may indicate that any letter claiming to be from him needed to be checked for the personal note before being accepted as genuine (cf. 2 Thessalonians 2:2).

which is the token in every epistle: so I write.—These words emphasize the fact that Paul's personal writing is a "token" or "mark" used to refer to "that which distinguishes a person or thing from others" (G. Abbott-Smith). "So I write" seems to mean "this is how I write" rather than indicating a custom of Paul's because he did not place his signature, or autograph, on all his letters.

V:18 The grace of our Lord Jesus Christ be with you all.— Apart from the use of the word "all," the second epistle ends as the first one. Paul does use the word "all" in other benedictions. But it certainly shows that he did not want to leave anyone out of his prayer for the Lord's blessing.

SELECTED BIBLIOGRAPHY

LEXICONS

Abbott-Smith, G. *A Manual Greek Lexicon of the New Testament.* Edinburgh: T. & T. Clark, 1964 reprint.

Bauer, Walter. *A Greek-English Lexicon of the New Testament and Other Early Christian Literature.* 2nd ed. revised by William F. Arndt, F. Wilbur Gingrich, and Frederick W. Danker. Chicago: University of Chicago Press, 1979.

Louw, Johannes P. and Nida, Eugene A. eds. *Greek-English Lexicon of the New Testament.* 2 vols. New York: United Bible Societies, 1988.

COMMENTARIES

Bruce, F. F. *1 and 2 Thessalonians.* Word Biblical Commentary, vol. 45. Waco, Texas: Word Books, Publishers, 1982.

Ellingworth, Paul and Nida, Eugene A. *A Translator's Handbook on Paul's Letters to the Thessalonians.* New York: United Bible Societies, 1976.

Fields, Wilbur. *Thinking Through Thessalonians.* Bible Study Textbook. Joplin, Missouri: College Press, 1963.

Findlay, G. G. *The Epistles of Paul the Apostle to the Thessalonians.* Cambridge Greek Testament for Schools and Colleges. Cambridge: University Press, 1904.

Frame, James E. *A Critical and Exegetical Commentary on the Epistles of St. Paul to the Thessalonians.* International Critical Commentary. Edinburgh: T. & T. Clark, 1912.

Hendriksen, William. *Exposition of 1 and 2 Thessalonians.* Grand Rapids: Baker Book House, 1955.

Hogg, C. F. and Vine, W. E. *The Epistles to the Thessalonians.* Grand Rapids: Kregel Publications, 1959 reprint.

Kelcy, Raymond C. *The Letters of Paul to the Thessalonians.* The Living Word Commentary. Austin: R. B. Sweet Co., Inc., 1968.

Lenski, R. C. H. *The Interpretation of St. Paul's Epistles to the Colossians, to the Thessalonians, to Timothy, to Titus and to Philemon.* Minneapolis: Augsburg Publishing House, 1964 reprint.

Lightfoot, J. B. *Notes on the Epistles of St. Paul: 1 and 2 Thessalonians, 1 Corinthians 1-7, Romans 1-7, Ephesians 1:1-14.* Grand Rapids: Zondervan Publishing House, 1957 reprint.

Lipscomb, David and Shepherd, J. W. *1 and 2 Thessalonians, 1 and 2 Timothy, Titus, and Philemon.* A Commentary on the New Testament Epistles. Nashville: Gospel Advocate Company, 1942.

McGarvey, J. W. and Pendleton, Philip Y. *Thessalonians, Corinthians, Galatians and Romans.* Cincinnati: The Standard Publishing Company, 1916.

Marshall, I. Howard. *1 and 2 Thessalonians.* The New Century Bible. Grand Rapids: Wm. B. Eerdmans Publishing Co., 1983.

Moffatt, James. *The First and Second Epistles to the Thessalonians.* The Expositor's Greek Testament. London: Hodder and Stoughton, MCMX.

Neil, William. *The Epistle of Paul to the Thessalonians.* London: Hodder and Stoughton, 1950.

Thomas, Robert L. "1 and 2 Thessalonians," in *The Expositor's Bible Commentary,* vol. 11. Grand Rapids: Zondervan Publishing House, 1978.

Ward, Ronald A. *Commentary on 1 and 2 Thessalonians.* Waco, Texas: Word Books, Publisher, 1980 reprint.